French

Visual Dictionary

for dummies®

WILEY

French Visual Dictionary For Dummies®

Published by
John Wiley & Sons, Inc.
111 River St.
Hoboken, NJ 07030-5774
www.wiley.com

For general information on our other products and services, or how to create a custom *For Dummies* book for your business or organization, please contact our Business Development Department in the U.S. at 877-409-4177, contact info@dummies.biz, or visit www.wiley.com/go/custompub. For information about licensing the *For Dummies* brand for products or services, contact BrandedRights&Licenses@Wiley.com.

Library of Congress Control Number: 2021933246

ISBN: 978-1-119-71719-5; ePDF: 978-1-119-71701-0; ePub: 978-1-119-71725-6

SKY10025772_062221

Table of Contents

En route !

Let's go! 15

Les transports / Transportation 16

La communication de base

Basic Communication 41

Dire bonjour / Saying hello 42

S'orienter

Orienting yourself 49

En ville / In the city 50

Dans la nature / The natural world 66

Bon appétit !

Enjoy your meal! 79

Qu'est-ce qu'on mange ? / What's there to eat? 80

Au restaurant / At the restaurant 113

Quelques plats / Some dishes 119

Les boissons / Drinks 126

Bonne nuit!

Good night! 133

Les hébergements / Accommodations 134
Dans la chambre / In the bedroom 157
Dans la salle de bains / In the bathroom 163

Les sorties!

Let's go out! 169

Parler d'argent / Talking about money 170
Les commerces / The shops 183
Le shopping / Shopping 191
Le sport / Sports 212
La culture / Culture 222

En cas d'urgence

In case of emergencies 245

Les accidents / Accidents 246
Les urgences / Emergencies 253

Introduction

This *Visual Dictionary For Dummies* is your ideal travel companion. It can be carried conveniently and consulted quickly; all you have to do is show the picture of the thing you're talking about or of the situation you wish to describe, and presto! And since the pictures are accompanied by the corresponding English words and their French translations, you will also be able to learn a lot of new vocabulary!

Sounds, rhythm and intonation

French and English have a lot in common, including a common history. French is a Romance language descended from Latin with German and English influences, while English is a Germanic language peppered with French and Latin borrowings. Thus, they share some similarities, most notably the same alphabet and a number of true cognates — words that are the same in both French and English, such as **original**, **final**, and **mental**.

The sounds: the vowels

Simple vowels

In English, the vowels are divided into two groups: the so-called long or tense vowels and the so-called short or lax vowels. French has a similar system, with a few twists. For example, vowels in French are what are known as *pure vowels;* that is to say they are not diphthongs as in British and American English. Most English speakers pronounce the letters "a" and "e" with an extra *yuh* sound at the end, and their "o's" and "u's" with an extra *wuh* sound at the end. You must not do this in French.

The distinction between long and short vowels exists in French, but two of the English short vowels do not exist (the short "i" in **did** and the short "u" in **put**) so make sure to never pronounce these vowels when speaking French.

Here's a listing of the vowel sounds found in French:

- **acheter (short a):** The French sound in **acheter** is kind of like American English's short "o" sound, as in **hot**, but in French the lips are spread more widely. It may be spelled A or À (an *accent grave*). In one word — **femme** — it is spelled with an "e."

Only three French vowels can take the *accent grave*: à, è, and ù. The purpose of the accent depends on the letter in question, although it generally indicates that the vowel should be short.

- **pâtes (long a):** This sound is pronounced with more rounded lips and is slightly elongated; it falls somewhere between the French short "a" and the "au" sound in the English word **pauper**.

REMEMBER

The *accent circonflexe* (here on the **â**) can be found on a, e, i, o, or u. It often means that, in the original Latin form of the word, the vowel was followed by the letter "s." It can be used to distinguish between two words — **sur** (on) versus **sûr** (sure), for example — or to change pronunciation.

- **école (long e):** The French "e" sound in **école** matches the sound we have for the "a" in **gate**. The annoying thing about the long "e" sound is that there are at least 6 different spellings for this sound in addition to the **é** in **école**:
  - *er*: At the end of an infinitive verb (*chanter*)
  - *ez*: Second person plural verb ending (*vous chàntez*)
  - *ez*: At the end of a word (*nez*)
  - *e (ss)*: At the beginning of a word (*essence*)
  - *ed*: At the end of a word (*pied*)
  - *e (ff)*: At the beginning of a word (*effort*)

REMEMBER

The *accent aigu* (**é,** acute accent) can only be added to the letter "e." At the beginning of a word, "é" is usually a sort of linguistic marker, indicating that the Old French or Latin word started with es or s. For example, you can trace the French word **école** back to the Middle French **escole** and the Latin **schola**.

- **pêche (short e):** To get the short French "e" sound, just think of the "e" sound in **pet**. Again, the one sound has multiple additional spellings:
  - *è*: nouns, adjectives, and so on (*mère*)
  - *e*: before a consonant (*elle*)
  - *ei*: nouns, adjectives, and so on (*reine*)
  - *et*: at the end of a word (*carnet*)
  - *ai*: nouns, adjectives, and so on (*raisin*)
  - *aî*: nouns, adjectives, and so on (*maître*)
- **(short i):** Don't worry about the short "i" sound. It doesn't exist in French.
- **petit (long i):** Think **ski** when you want to say a long French "i" sound.
- **sonner (short o):** The sound of the French **sonner** is a good match for the short "o" sound in the English word **not**.
- **rose (long o):** The sound of the French **rose** is similar to English's long "o" sound as in **go**, but without the diphthong transition to a "w" sound at the end.
- **(short u):** Don't worry about the short "u" sound. It doesn't exist in French.
- **loupe (long u):** The long "u" sound in French closely matches the vowel sound we have in the English word **boot**.

- **samedi (e instable or e muet/schwa):** In French, words like **samedi** can be pronounced two ways — as a three-syllable word (*sahm-uh-dee*) or a two-syllable word (*sahm-dee*). As a three-syllable word, you have a long "a" sound in the first syllable and an *unaccented schwa* sound in the second syllable. ("Unaccented" here just means that you don't emphasize that syllable at all; the "schwa" sound is, believe it or not, the most common vowel sound in the English language.) For the second syllable (the *schwa* syllable), think of the sound in the English word **uh** — that word we say when we are trying to think of a word — or the last syllable in a word like **banana**.

Blending your words

Yes, French speakers tend to talk fast! That means words tend to blend together — you sometimes don't make a clear distinction from the end of one word and the beginning of another:

- **Vowel/Vowel:** When a word ends with a vowel and the following word also starts with a vowel, both vowels form two syllables, and you don't add a pause.
- For example, with the phrase **Tu as un vélo** ("You have a bike"), you'd say the entire phrase as if it were one word without any pauses, and the sounds of **Tu as** seem to merge.
- **Consonant/Vowel:** When a word ends with a consonant and the following word starts with a vowel, the

last consonant of the first word becomes the first letter of the second word, as in **Il arrive** ("he arrives"), pronounced "eelareev." You link the consonant to the vowel to form a syllable.

The sounds: the consonants

Most French consonants match the sound of English exactly, but you'll need to pay particular attention to some consonants that are tricky for English speakers to pronounce.

- **"c":** In French, the letter "c" has two pronunciations — hard and soft. The hard pronunciation (**le cadeau**) uses the "c" sound found in the English word **carrot**. The soft pronunciation (**une cerise**) uses the "c" sound found in the English word **ceremony**. Use the soft pronunciation when the "c" comes right before an "e," "i," or "y." Use the hard pronunciation when the "c" comes right before an "a," "o," or "u."

REMEMBER

When a "c" precedes a hard vowel but needs a soft pronunciation (in the case of **ça va?**, for example), you change the "c" to a "ç" (*cédille*) to make the "c" soft.

- **"ch":** The French "ch" (**chien**) almost always has the "sh" sound found in the English name **Sherlock**. The "ch" sound in the English word **cheese** only occurs in words borrowed from English, like **cheap** and **le match**. The only other pronunciation you might run across is the "k" sound you find in the word **le chaos** — it appears in the English word **chaos** as well.

- **"g":** Just like the French "c," the French "g" has two pronunciations — hard and soft. The hard pronunciation (**le gare**) uses the "g" sound found in the English word **gold**. The soft pronunciation (**gérer**) uses the "g" sound found in the English word **massage**. Again, use the soft pronunciation when the "g" comes right before an "e," "i," or "y." Use the hard pronunciation when the "g" comes right before an "a," "o," or "u."

REMEMBER

When a "g" precedes an "e," "i," or "y," but needs a soft pronunciation, you add a "u" to make it soft (**guérir**, for example). When a "g" precedes an "a," "o," or "u," but needs a hard pronunciation, you add an "e" to make it hard (**nous mangeons**, for example).

- **"h":** The letter "h" is always silent in French, as in **l'homme**, **heureux**, and **haut**.
- **"j":** The French "j" is always soft. In fact, it sounds exactly like the soft French "g" in **gérer**. So, if you can pronounce the "g" sound in an English word like **massage,** you can pronounce the French "j" in a word like **jeudi**.
- **"q":** For all intents and purposes, a "q" in French is going to be followed by a "u" — just like in English. In French, however, the "qu" combination can sound like an English "k" (as in **quand**) or it can have the "kw"

sound found in the English word **quiz** (think **l'équateur** or **l'aquarelle**.)

The one exception to the "q followed by u" rule is when a French word ends in "q," as in **cinq** and **le coq**.

- **"r":** The French "guttural R" (**rouge**) poses particular problems for English speakers, since the sound doesn't really exist in the English language. The closest we come is when we try to imitate a dog by saying **Grrrrrr, grrrrrrrr!** The idea is to get that throaty, guttural sound and put it at the front of the word — kind of like the **rrrrruff rrrrrruff** English speakers use to imitate a dog barking.
- **"s":** The letter "s" in French has two distinct pronunciations — just like English, by the way. Think of the "s" sound in **sensibility** versus the "s" sound found in the word **vision**. In French, the "s" sound is almost always the **sensibility** sound; the **vision** sound only occurs when you have a single "s" between two vowels (**visage**) or when you are blending two words (**ils ont**).
- **"th":** The "th" sound found in an English word like **theater** does not exist in French. That means a word like **le thé** starts with the same "t" sound as the English word **tea**.

The non-sounds: silent letters

French words end with all kinds of letters that, to English speakers, seem to be randomly pronounced or ignored. However, it's not as random as it appears. Here are some tips to help you understand when letters should be silent.

- **C, R, F, L:** If a French word ends with "c," "r," "l," or "f," the final letter is usually pronounced.

  - **Un truc**
  - **Un dortoir**
  - **Le chef**
  - **Avril**

  There's one big exception to the CRFL rule: Verbs ending with the letters "er" have a silent "r."

  - **Aimer**
  - **Manger**
  - **Tuer**

- **B, K, Q:** In addition to the CRFL words, words ending with "b," "k," and "q" also have their final letter pronounced.

  - **Le club**
  - **Un steak**
  - **Cinq**

All other consonant letters found at the end of words are usually *not* pronounced:

- **Froid (*exceptions: sud, proper names like David and Alfred*)**
- **Le poing (*exceptions: le grog*)**
- **Un dragon (*exceptions: amen*)**
- **Le parfum (*exceptions: aquarium or forum*)**
- **Un coup (*exceptions: un slip, un cap*)**
- **Le marais (*exceptions: un fils, un autobus, le tennis*)**
- **Elle mangeait (*exceptions: brut, huit, words ending in -ct and-pt, like direct and sept*)**
- **Deux (*exceptions: six, index, Aix*)**
- **Le riz (*exceptions: le gaz*)**

REMEMBER

The logic behind the one exception to the "M" rule has to do with French words taken straight from the Latin — like **aquarium** or **forum**, as pointed out above. In such cases, the final "m" is pronounced.

En route !

Let's go!

À l'aéroport

At the airport

Aéroport
Airport

Compagnie aérienne
Airline

Comptoir d'enregistrement
Check-in counter

Sécurité
Security

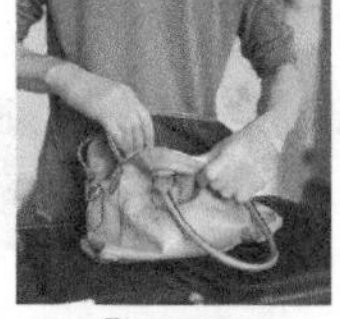

Douanes
Customs

Vol
Flight

Panneau d'affichage
Departure/Arrival board

Correspondance
Connecting flight

Bagage à main
Hand/Carry-on luggage

Bagages
Luggage, baggage

Valise
Suitcase

Sac à dos
Backpack

À l'aéroport

At the airport

Chariot (à bagages)
(Luggage) trolley

Récupération des bagages
Baggage claim

Passeport
Passport

Billet
Ticket

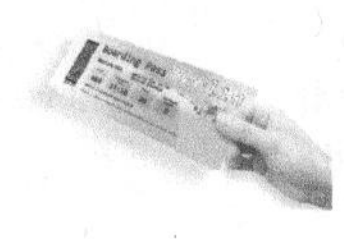

Carte d'embarquement
Boarding pass

Porte d'embarquement
Gate

Embarquement
Boarding

À l'aéroport

At the airport

Phrases clés	Key phrases
Merci de présenter votre passeport et votre carte d'embarquement à la porte d'embarquement.	Please present your passport and boarding pass at the gate.
Veuillez sortir votre ordinateur portable de votre sac à la sécurité.	Please take your laptop out of your bag at security.
Le vol AF22 pour Paris est prêt pour l'embarquement.	Flight AF22 to Paris is now ready to board.
Dernier appel pour les passagers du vol BA354 à destination de Nice.	This is the final call for passengers on flight BA354 to Nice.

L'avion

The plane

Steward/Hôtesse de l'air
Flight attendant

Pilote
Pilot

Siège
Seat

Ceinture de sécurité
Seat belt

Hublot
Window

Couloir
Aisle

Piste
Runway

Sortie de secours
Emergency exit

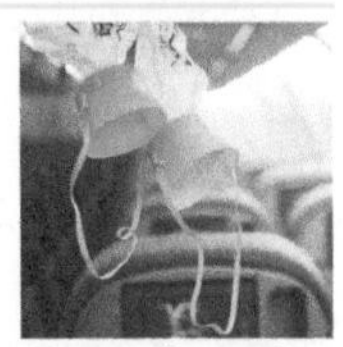

Masque à oxygène
Oxygen mask

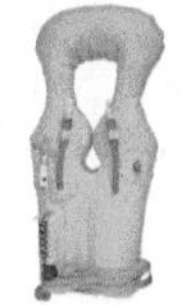

Gilet de sauvetage
Life vest

Décoller
To take off

Atterrir
To land

L'avion
The plane

Aile
Wing

Moteur, réacteur
Engine

Toilettes
Bathroom, lavatory

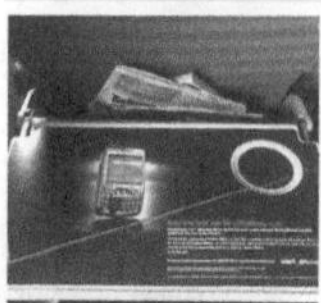

Tablette
Tray table

L'avion

The plane

Phrases clés	Key phrases
Veuillez attacher votre ceinture de sécurité.	Please fasten your seat belt.
Nous vous rappelons que ce vol est non-fumeur.	We remind you that this is a non-smoking flight.
Nous allons vous montrer les consignes de sécurité.	We will be showing our safety demonstration.
Tous les appareils électroniques doivent être en mode avion ou éteints.	All electronic devices must be switched to airplane mode or switched off.
Veuillez vous assurer que le dossier de votre siège est remonté et que votre tablette est rangée.	Please make sure your seat backs and tray tables are in their full upright position.

Le train
The train

Gare
Train station

Train
Train

Voie (ferrée)
(Railway) track

Quai
Platform

Train à grande vitesse
High-speed train

Compartiment
Compartment

Voiture, wagon
Carriage, coach, car

Wagon-restaurant
Dining-car

Wagon-lit
Sleeping-car

Passage à niveau
Level crossing

Guichet
Booking/Ticket office

Billetterie automatique
Ticket machine

Le train
The train

Aller simple
Single/One-way ticket

Aller-retour
Return/Round-trip ticket

Consigne
Left luggage office, checkroom

Bureau d'informations
Information desk

Contrôleur
Ticket inspector

Train de nuit
Overnight train

Couchettes
Berths

Tarif
Fare

Composter (un billet)
To punch (a ticket)

Monter dans le train
To get on the train

Descendre du train
To get off the train

Le train

The train

Phrases clés	Key phrases
Je souhaiterais acheter un aller simple pour Marseilles.	I'd like to buy a single ticket to Marseilles.
À quelle heure part le prochain train pour Nantes ?	When does the next train for Nantes leave?
Le train à destination de Paris dessert les gares de Rouen et Giverny.	The train to Paris stops at Rouen and Giverny.
Le train en provenance de Calais entre en gare voie 2.	The train from Calais is arriving at platform 2.

Les transports en commun

Public transportation

Transports en commun
Public transportation

Bus
Bus

Autobus
Coach

Bus à impériale
Double-decker

Navette
Shuttle bus

Arrêt de bus
Bus stop

Chauffeur de bus
Bus driver

Prix du trajet
Fare

Siège
Seat

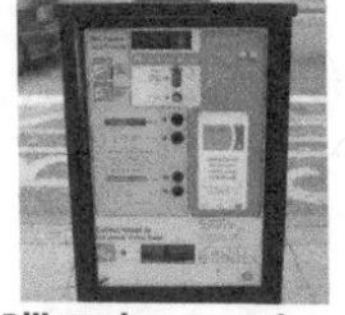

Billetterie automatique
Ticket machine

Carnet de tickets
Book of tickets

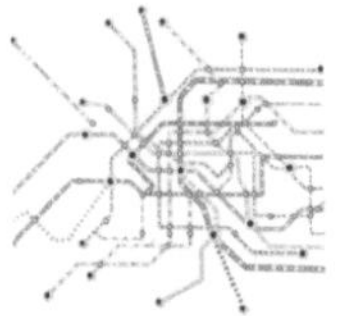

Itinéraire
Route

Les transports en commun

Public transportation

Métro
Underground (UK)/Subway (US)

Station de métro
Underground/Subway station

Train de banlieue
Commuter/Local train

Tramway
Tram

Quai
Platform

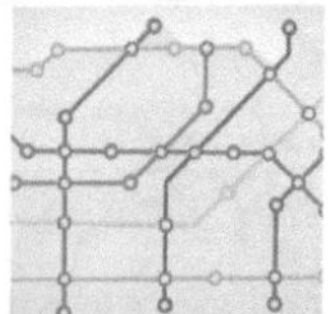

Réseau
Network

Ligne
Line

Présenter son ticket
To produce one's ticket

Rater le bus
To miss the bus

Les transports en commun

Public transportation

Phrases clés	Key phrases
Où est l'arrêt de bus le plus proche ?	Where is the nearest bus stop?
Quel bus dois-je prendre pour aller à l'aéroport ?	What bus do I take to get to the airport?
À quelle heure le bus part-il ?	What time does the bus leave?
Dois-je descendre ici pour aller au musée ?	Do I get off here for the museum?
Combien y a-t-il d'arrêts pour aller à la plage ?	How many stops are there to go to the beach?
Prendre le métro aux heures de pointe est une mauvaise idée : c'est bondé !	Riding the subway during peak hour is a bad idea: it is crammed!

La voiture

The car

Voiture
Car

Permis de conduire
Driving licence, driver's license (US)

Réservoir
Tank

Essence
Petrol, gas (US)

Station essence
Petrol/Gas station

Voiture de location
Rental car

Phares avant
Headlights

Feux arrière
Tail lights

Feux de stop
Brake lights

Feux de détresse
Warning lights

Moteur
Engine

Ceinture de sécurité
Safety belt

La voiture

The car

Carrosserie
Body

Portière
Door

Pare-brise
Windscreen, windshield (US)

Pare-chocs
Bumper

Capot
Bonnet, hood (US)

Coffre
Boot, trunk (US)

Roue de secours
Spare wheel

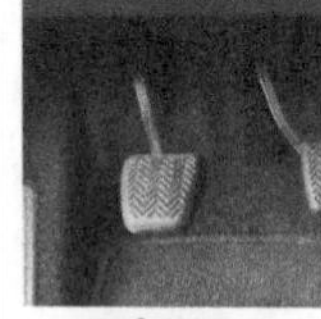

Embrayage
Clutch

Frein
Brake

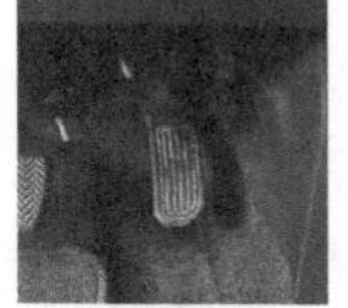

Accélérateur
Accelerator

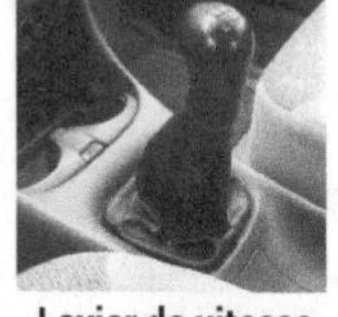

Levier de vitesse
Gear lever, gear shift (US)

Volant
Steering wheel

La voiture

The car

Clignotant
Indicator, turn signal

Rétroviseur
Rear-view mirror

Jauge de carburant
Fuel gauge

Indicateur de vitesse
Speedometer

Tableau de bord
Dashboard

Rétroviseur extérieur
Wing mirror, side-view mirror

Klaxon
Horn

Boîte à gants
Glove compartment

Poignée de porte
Door handle

Frein à main
Handbrake,
emergency brake (US)

Pot d'échappement
Exhaust, tail pipe

Pneu
Tyre, tire (US)

La voiture

The car

Roue
Wheel

Plaque d'immatriculation
Number plate, license plate (US)

Embouteillage
Traffic jam

Panne
Breakdown

Trousse à outils
Tool kit

Cric
Jack

Batterie
Battery

Serrure
Lock

Réseau routier
Road network

Autoroute
Highway

Autoroute à péage
Motorway, turnpike (US)

Parking
Car park, parking lot (US)

La voiture

The car

Horodateur, parcmètre
Parking meter

Parking à étages
Multi-story car park

Se garer en double file
To double-park

Amende pour stationnement
Parking ticket

Impasse, voie sans issue
Dead end, no through road

Passage piétons
Pedestrian/Zebra crossing

Vitesse maximale autorisée
Speed limit

Panneau de signalisation
Road sign

Feux de signalisation
Traffic lights, stop lights

Carrefour
Crossroads

Rue à sens unique
One-way street

Sortie
Exit

La voiture

The car

Péage

Toll

Conduire

To drive

Se garer

To park

Faire marche arrière

To reverse

Dépasser, doubler

To overtake, to pass

Avoir un accident

To smash, to crash

Faire le plein d'essence

To fill up

La voiture

The car

Phrases clés	Key phrases
Où est la station service la plus proche ?	Where is the nearest gas station?
Y a-t-il un parking dans le coin ?	Is there a car park around here?
Ma voiture est tombée en panne.	My car has broken down.
Le moteur ne veut pas démarrer.	The engine won't start.
La batterie est à plat.	The battery is dead.
Je dois emmener la voiture chez le garagiste.	I need to take the car to the garage.

Le taxi

The taxi

Taxi
Taxi, cab

Chauffeur de taxi
Taxi/Cab driver, cabbie (UK)

Course de taxi
Taxi ride

Station de taxi
Taxi rank/stand

Prix de la course
Taxi fare

Compteur
Meter

Héler un taxi
To hail a cab

Le taxi

The taxi

Phrases clés	Key phrases
Où puis-je trouver une station de taxi ?	Where can I find a taxi stand?
Puis-je réserver un taxi pour 9 heures pour aller à l'aéroport ?	May I book a taxi at 9am to go to the airport?
Il faut passer me prendre à mon hôtel.	I need to be picked up at my hotel.
Je suis pressé, pouvez-vous prendre le chemin le plus rapide ?	I'm in a hurry, can you take the quickest route?
Peut-on passer devant la Cathédrale sur le chemin ?	Can we drive past the cathedral on the way?
À combien s'élève la course, s'il vous plaît ?	How much is the fare, please?
Gardez la monnaie.	Keep the change.

Le vélo
The bike

Vélo
Bike

Guidon
Handlebar

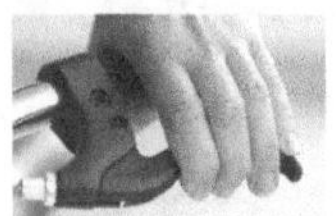

Freins
Brakes

Roue
Wheel

Levier de vitesse
Shift lever, gear shifter

Selle
Saddle

Pneu
Tyre, tire (US)

Chambre à air
Inner tube

Crevaison
Puncture, flat

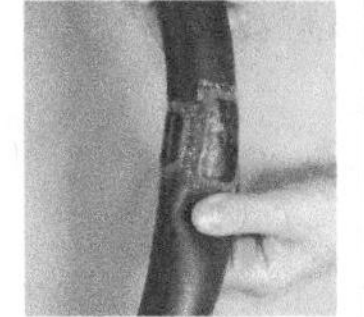

Rustine
Patch

Pédale
Pedal

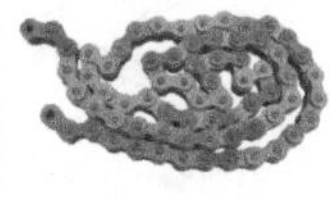

Chaîne
Chain

Le vélo
The bike

Panier
Basket

Sonnette
Bell

Casque de vélo
Bicycle helmet

Béquille
Kickstand

Éclairage
Lighting

Antivol
Bike lock

Garde-boue
Mudguard

Réflecteurs
Reflector

Petites roues, roues stabilisatrices
Training wheels

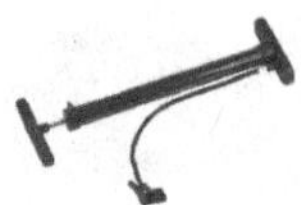

Pompe à vélo
Bicycle pump

Range-vélos
Bicycle rack

Piste cyclable
Bicycle lane

Le vélo
The bike

Faire du vélo
To ride a bike

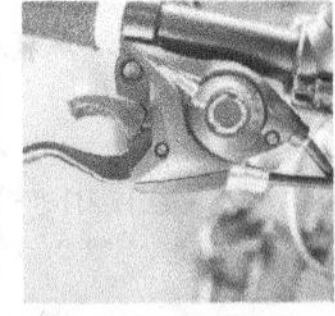

Changer de vitesse
To shift gears

Freiner
To brake

Le vélo

The bike

Phrases clés	Key phrases
Y a-t-il un magasin de vélo dans le coin ?	Is there a bike shop around here?
J'aimerais louer un vélo pour trois jours.	I would like to rent a bike for three days.
Il est obligatoire de porter un casque.	Wearing a helmet is mandatory.
J'ai un pneu crevé.	I have a flat tire.
Veuillez rester sur la piste cyclable.	Please stay on the bicycle lane.

La communication de base

Basic Communication

Dire bonjour

Saying hello

Bonjour
Hello, hi

Bonjour (le matin)
Good morning

Bonjour (l'après-midi), bon après-midi
Good afternoon

Bonsoir
Good evening

Bonne nuit
Good night

Phrases clés	Key phrases
Comment vas-tu/allez-vous ?	How are you (doing)?
Comment ça va ?	How is it going?
Et toi/vous ?	What about you?
Je vais bien.	I'm fine.
Enchanté(e) de faire votre connaissance.	How do you do?
Ravi(e) de te/vous rencontrer.	Nice/Pleased to meet you.
Quoi de neuf ?	What's up?

Demander poliment

Asking politely

Phrases clés	Key phrases
Pouvez-vous s'il vous plaît … ?	Can you please … ?
Pouvez-vous me dire où se trouve la gare s'il vous plaît ?	Can you please tell me where the train station is?
Je cherche …	I am looking for …
Je cherche le supermarché.	I am looking for the supermarket.
J'aimerais …	I would like to …
J'aimerais acheter deux places pour le spectacle.	I would like to buy two tickets for the show.
Puis-je vous demander comment … ?	May I ask you how to … ?
Puis-je vous demander comment se rendre à la plage ?	May I ask you how to go to the beach?
Puis-je avoir … ?	Could/May I have … ?
Puis-je avoir votre numéro, s'il vous plaît ?	Could I have your number, please?

Demander poliment

Asking politely

Pourriez-vous s'il vous plaît ... ?	Could you please ... ?
Pourriez-vous me montrer où nous sommes sur le plan s'il vous plaît ?	Could you please show me where we are on the map?
Cela vous dérangerait-il de ... ?	Would you mind ... ?
Cela vous dérangerait-il de fermer la porte ?	Would you mind closing the door?
Auriez-vous l'amabilité de ... ?	Would you be so kind as to ... ?
Auriez-vous l'amabilité de nous dire à quelle heure ouvre le musée ?	Would you be so kind as to tell us when the museum opens?

Remercier
Thanking

Merci
Thank you

De rien, je vous en prie
You're welcome

Phrases clés	Key phrases
Merci beaucoup !	Thank you very much!
Merci pour tout !	Thanks for everything!
Comment pourrais-je vous remercier suffisamment ?	How can I ever thank you enough?
C'est tellement gentil de votre part !	That's so sweet of you!
Merci beaucoup de votre aide !	Thank you so much for your help!
Tout le plaisir est pour moi.	It's my pleasure.
N'en parlons plus !	Don't mention it!
Inutile de me remercier.	You don't have to thank me.

Dire au revoir

Saying goodbye

Au revoir
Bye, goodbye

À un de ces jours
So long

À la prochaine
See you later

À bientôt
See you soon

Phrases clés	Key phrases
Bonne journée !	Have a good day!
Je dois y aller.	I've got to go now.
Je ferais bien de partir.	I'd better go.
C'était un plaisir de vous rencontrer.	It was nice meeting you.
Je me suis bien amusé(e).	I had a great time.
Bon retour.	Have a safe trip back.
Bonne fin de journée.	Enjoy the rest of your day.

S'excuser

Apologizing

Désolé
Sorry

Excusez-moi
Excuse me

Phrases clés	Key phrases
Je suis désolé(e).	I'm sorry.
Je m'excuse !	I apologize!
Je te/vous prie de m'excuser.	I beg your pardon.
Je te/vous prie de bien vouloir m'excuser.	Please forgive me.
Je suis sincèrement désolé(e).	I'm terribly sorry.
J'aimerais m'excuser pour mon erreur.	I would like to apologize for my mistake.
Je te/vous prie de bien vouloir accepter mes excuses.	Please accept my sincere apologies.
N'en parlons plus.	Let's forget about it.
C'est pardonné.	It's forgiven.

S'orienter

Orienting yourself

Demander sur un plan

Asking on a map

Plan, carte
Map

Directions
Directions

Être perdu
To be lost

Phrases clés	Key phrases
Je cherche ...	I am looking for ...
Excusez-moi, savez-vous où se trouve la gare routière ?	Excuse me, do you know where the bus station is?
Pouvez-vous me dire comment me rendre à Big Ben ?	Could you tell me how to get to Big Ben?
Pouvez-vous me l'indiquer sur la carte ?	Can you show me on the map?
À quelle distance se trouve Versailles ?	How far is Versailles from here?
Quel est le meilleur chemin pour aller à Oxford ?	What is the best way to go to Oxford?

Les directions

Directions

Tout droit
Straight

Gauche
Left

Droite
Right

Côté gauche
Left-hand side

Côté droit
Right-hand side

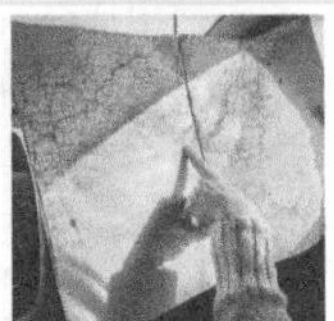

Où ?
Where?

Près
Near, close to

Loin
Far

Ici
Here

Là-bas
There

En direction de
Towards

Devant
In front of

Les directions
Directions

Derrière
Behind

Suivre
To follow

Tourner
To turn

Traverser
To cross

Faire demi-tour
To turn back

Les directions

Directions

Phrases clés	Key phrases
Le cinéma est sur le côté droit de la rue.	The cinema is on the right-hand side of the street.
Au carrefour, tournez à gauche.	At the crossroads, make a left.
Tournez à gauche sur la Rue de Rivoli puis allez tout droit.	Turn left into Rue de Rivoli then go straight on.
Prenez la première rue sur la droite.	Take the first street on the right.
Pour aller au parc, suivez les panneaux.	To go to the park, follow the signs.
La cathédrale est à l'autre bout de la rue, faites demi-tour.	The cathedral is at the other end of the street, turn around.
Le restaurant est proche de l'hôtel.	The restaurant is near the hotel.
La plupart des bars sont situés le long du fleuve.	Most of the bars are located alongside the river.

Les rues et quartiers

Streets and districts

Grande rue
High street, main street

Impasse
Cul-de-sac, dead end street

Route
Road

Rue
Street

Rue à sens unique
One-way street

Boulevard
Boulevard

Avenue
Avenue

Ruelle
Lane

Chemin de terre
Path

Trottoir
Pavement, sidewalk

Zone piétonne
Pedestrian area

Carrefour
Crossroads

Les rues et quartiers

Streets and districts

Centre-ville
Downtown, city center

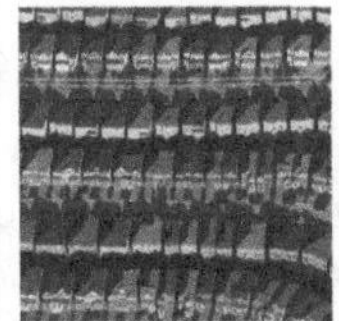

Banlieue
Suburb

Appartement
Flat, apartment

Résidence
Block of flats/apartments

Gratte-ciel
Skyscraper, high-rise building

Capitale
Capital

Grand centre urbain, métropole
Metropolis

Ville
Town

Cité, grande ville
City

Quartier
District

Les rues et quartiers

Streets and districts

Phrases clés	Key phrases
Notre hôtel se trouve dans le centre-ville de Nice.	Our hotel is in downtown Nice.
Il y a un quartier algérienne dans la plupart des grandes villes aux France.	There is an Algerian quarter in most cities in France.
Les plus grands centres commerciaux se trouvent dans les banlieues.	The biggest shopping centers are located in the suburbs.
L'appartement que nous louions était dans un gratte-ciel.	The apartment we were renting was in a high-rise building.
Il était difficile de conduire dans Paris à cause de toutes les rues à sens unique.	It was hard to drive around Paris because of all the one-way streets.

Les lieux importants
Significant places

Office de tourisme
Tourist information centre/center

Église
Church

Cathédrale
Cathedral

Mosquée
Mosque

Synagogue
Synagogue

Pagode
Pagoda

Mairie
City hall

Parlement
Parliament

Bibliothèque
Library

Musée
Museum

Galerie
Gallery

Château
Castle

Les lieux importants
Significant places

Place
Square

Parc
Park

Restaurant
Restaurant

Café
Pub, cafe

Salle de sport
Gym

Phare
Lighthouse

Quai (d'un fleuve)
Embankment

Monument aux morts
War memorial

Poste de police
Police station

Caserne de pompiers
Fire station

Poste, bureau de poste
Post office

Théâtre
Theatre, theater (US)

Les lieux importants

Significant places

Cinéma
Cinema

Foire, fête foraine
Fun fair, amusement fair

Cirque
Circus

Zoo
Zoo

Aquarium
Aquarium

La tour d'eifel
The Eiffel Tower

Notre-Dame de Paris
Notre Dame Cathedral

Château de Versailles
The Palace of Versailles

Les Champs-Élysées
Champs-Élysées Avenue

Le Arc de Triomphe de l'Étoile
The Arc de Triomphe

Le Mont-Saint-Michel
Mont-Saint-Michel

Chateau de Chambord
Chambord Palace

Les lieux importants
Significant places

Thermes de Bath
Roman Baths

Jardin de Luxembourg
Luxembourg Gardens

Centre Pompidou
Pompidou Center

Sainte-Chapelle
Sainte-Chapelle

Le Moulin Rouge
The Moulin Rouge

Le Louvre
The Louvre Museum

Le Musée d'Orsay
The Musée d'Orsay

Le Château de Chenonceau
Chenonceau Castle

Les lieux importants

Significant places

Phrases clés	Key phrases
Que recommendez-vous que nous visitions pendant nos vacances ?	What do you recommend we visit during our holiday?
Que pouvons-nous visiter avec des enfants ?	What can we visit with children?
L'office de tourisme est le lieu où vous pouvez trouver toutes les informations dont vous avez besoin pour vos visites.	The tourist information centre/center is where you can get all the information you need for your visits.
Les bâtiments religieux comprennent les églises, les cathédrales, les mosquées, les synagogues, les temples, les pagodes ...	Religious buildings include churches, cathedrals, mosques, synagogues, temples, pagodas ...
Les bibliothèques sont souvent des lieux majestueux.	Libraries are often magnificent places.

Les toilettes publiques

Public toilet

W.C.
Toilet, bathroom

Toilettes pour femmes
Ladies' room

Toilettes pour hommes
Men's room

Toilettes (informel)
Loo, john

Toilettes publiques
Public toilet

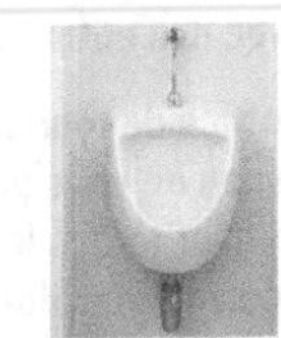

Urinoir
Urinal

Papier toilette
Toilet paper

Lavabo
Washbasin, bathroom sink

Savon pour les mains
Hand soap

Sèche-mains
Hand dryer

Table à langer
Changing table

Bouché
Clogged

Les toilettes publiques

Public toilet

Phrases clés	Key phrases
Excusez-moi, où sont les toilettes ?	Excuse me, where is the bathroom?
Y a-t-il des toilettes publiques près d'ici ?	Is there a public restroom nearby?
Pourriez-vous m'indiquer les toilettes pour femmes les plus proches ?	Could you direct me to the nearest ladies' room?
Y a-t-il une table à langer dans les toilettes publiques ?	Is there a changing table in the public toilet?
Ces toilettes sont hors d'usage, elles sont bouchées.	This bathroom is out of order, it's clogged.

Les directions

Directions

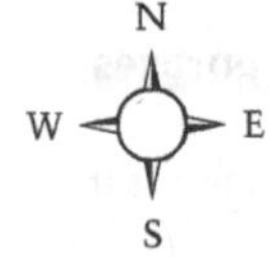

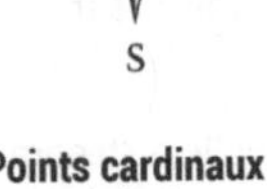

Points cardinaux
Cardinal points

Boussole
Compass

Nord
North

S

SUD

Sud
South

EST

Est
East

QUEST

Ouest
West

Les directions

Directions

Phrases clés	Key phrases
Tournez à l'ouest sur la Rue Gaspard Faraut pour arriver à la plage.	Turn west on Rue Gaspard Faraut to get to the beach.
Si vous continuez à marcher vers le nord, vous tomberez sur la gare.	If you keep walking northward, you'll find the train station.
Nice se trouve dans le sud de la France.	Nice is in the south of France.
La Bretagne se trouve sur la côte ouest de la France.	Brittany is on the western coast of France.
Pouvez-vous m'indiquer la direction du sud de la ville ?	Can you point me to the south of the city?

La météo

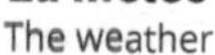

The weather

Météo
Weather

Prévisions météorologiques
Weather forecast

Température
Temperature

Printemps
Spring

Été
Summer

Automne
Autumn, fall

Hiver
Winter

Soleil
Sunshine

Sans nuage
Cloudless

Vague de chaleur
Heat wave

Brume de chaleur
Haze

Sécheresse
Drought

La météo

The weather

Lever de soleil
Sunrise

Coucher de soleil
Sunset

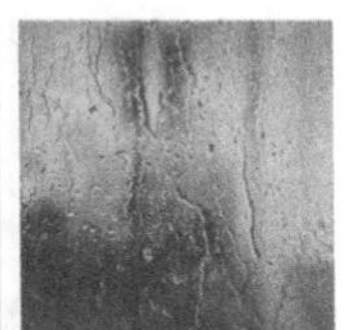

Pluie
Rain

Nuage
Cloud

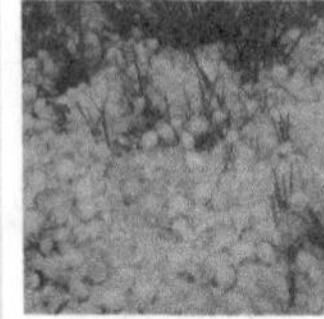

Grêle
Hail

Grêlon
Hailstone

Arc-en-ciel
Rainbow

Orage
Thunderstorm

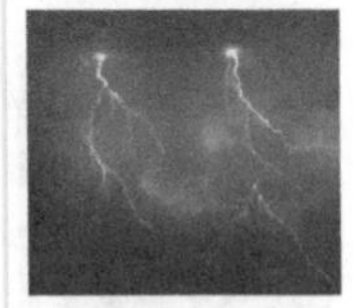

Tonnerre
Thunder

Éclair
Flash of lightning

Inondation
Flood

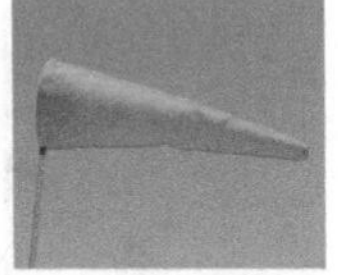

Vent
Wind

La météo

The weather

Tempête
Storm, tempest

Tornade
Tornado

Brouillard
Fog

Neige
Snow

Flocons de neige
Snowflakes

Volcan
Volcano

Éruption
Eruption

Lave
Lava

Tremblement de terre
Earthquake

Glissement de terrain
Landslide

Tempête de neige
Blizzard

Avalanche
Avalanche

La météo
The weather

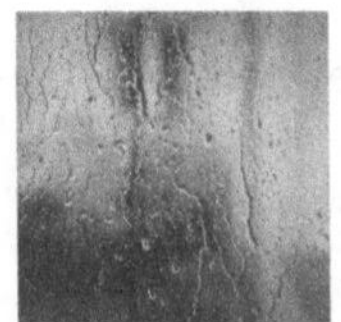

Pleuvoir
To rain

Souffler
To blow

Geler
To freeze

Neiger
To snow

La météo

The weather

Phrases clés	Key phrases
Quel temps fait-il ?	What is the weather like?
Il fait très chaud en Provence au mois de décembre.	It is hot in Provence in December.
L'automne est généralement frais et humide à Calais.	Autumn is usually chilly and damp in Calais.
On s'attend à ce que les températures se rafraîchissent cette semaine.	We are expecting the temperature to cool down this week.
Il fait beau, n'est-ce pas ?	Lovely day, isn't it?
Nous avons hâte que le temps se réchauffe.	We're looking forward to the weather warming up!
Nous aimons regarder les prévisions météo le matin pour planifier notre journée.	We like watching the weather forecast in the morning to plan our day.

La géographie et les paysages

Geography and landscapes

Paysage
Landscape

Panorama
Viewpoint, panorama

Côte
Coast

Océan
Ocean

Mer
Sea

Fleuve, rivière
River

Canal
Canal

Lac
Lake

Cascade, chute d'eau
Waterfall

Île
Island

Plage
Beach

Sable
Sand

La géographie et les paysages
Geography and landscapes

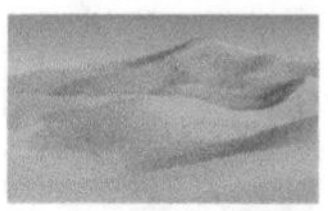

Dune
Dune

Falaise
Cliff

Rocher
Rock

Marée
Tide

Vague
Wave

Rive
Bank

Marais
Swamp, marsh

Plaine
Plain

Montagne
Mountain

Sommet
Summit

Glacier
Glacier

Vallée
Valley

La géographie et les paysages

Geography and landscapes

Colline
Hill

Caverne, grotte
Cave

Forêt
Forest

Jungle
Jungle

Désert
Desert

Canyon
Canyon

Volcan
Volcano

Ville
City

Campagne
Country

Champ
Field

Ferme
Farm

Savane
Bush

La géographie et les paysages

Geography and landscapes

Phrases clés	Key phrases
Je préfère aller à la plage plutôt qu'à la montagne.	I'd rather go to the beach than to the mountains.
Vérifie bien la marée avant d'aller à la plage.	Make sure you check the tide before going to the beach.
Passer du temps à la montagne en été est plus agréable parce que les températures sont plus basses.	Spending time in the mountains in the summer is nicer because the temperatures are lower.
Nous voulons vraiment plonger sur la *Côte d'Azur*.	We really want to dive along the Côte d'Azur.
Il y a des glaciers incroyables *Les Alpes françaises*.	There are amazing glaciers in the French Alps.

Quelques points de repère
Landmarks

Village
Village

Cimetière
Churchyard

Ferme
Farm

Forêt
Forest

Chemin de randonnée
Trail

Pont
Bridge

Piscine
Swimming pool

Stade
Stadium

École
School

Tribunal
Court

Prison
Prison

Caserne de pompiers
Fire station

Quelques points de repère
Landmarks

Poste de police
Police station

Hôpital
Hospital

Université
University

Centre culturel
Art centre/center

Statue
Statue

Fontaine
Fountain

Monument commémoratif
Memorial

Marché
Market

Banque
Bank

Quelques points de repère

Landmarks

Phrases clés	Key phrases
Le chemin de randonnée commence directement à la sortie du village.	The trail starts right on the outskirts of the village.
Tournez à gauche après le pont puis continuez tout droit jusqu'à ce que vous arriviez au marché.	Turn left after the bridge then go straight until you reach the market.
C'est plus court de passer à travers la forêt pour aller à la piscine.	It is shorter to get to the swimming pool if you pass through the forest.
Je cherche le centre culturel. Pouvez-vous me dire où il se trouve ?	I'm looking for the art centre/center. Can you tell me where it is?
Y a-t-il un marché aux alentours ?	Is there a market around here?

Bon appétit !

Enjoy your meal!

Les différents repas
Meals

Petit déjeuner
Breakfast

Déjeuner
Lunch

Dîner
Dinner

Brunch
Brunch

Souper
Supper

Repas
Meal

Plat, service
Course

Snack, casse-croûte
Snack

Manger
To eat

Boire
To drink

Avoir faim
To be hungry

Avoir soif
To be thirsty

Les différents repas
Meals

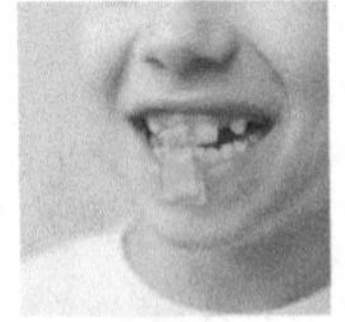

Mâcher
To chew

Faire cuire, cuisiner
To cook

Phrases clés	Key phrases
J'ai tellement faim, j'ai hâte de dîner.	I'm so hungry, I can't wait to have dinner.
Je préfère manger de la nourriture salée pour le petit déjeuner.	I prefer to eat savory food for breakfast.
Ne mange pas si vite et mâche ta nourriture correctement !	Don't eat so fast, and chew your food properly!

Les viandes/les poissons/les fruits de mer

Meat/fish/seafood

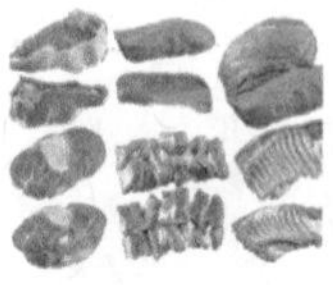 **Viande** Meat	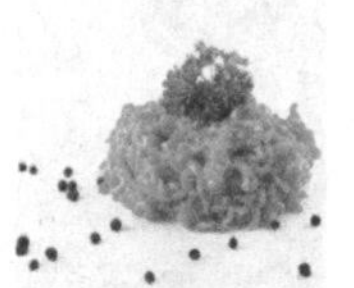 **Viande hachée** Hamburger meat	 **Bœuf** Beef
 **Porc** Pork	 **Agneau** Lamb	 **Mouton** Mutton
 **Veau** Veal	 **Poulet** Chicken	 **Dinde** Turkey
 **Lapin** Rabbit	 **Canard** Duck	 **Gibier** Venison

Les viandes/les poissons/les fruits de mer

Meat/fish/seafood

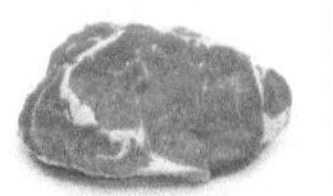

Steak
Steak

Bavette
Flank steak

Côte de porc
Pork chop

Côtelette
Chop, cutlet

Blanc de poulet
Chicken breast

Aile de poulet
Chicken wing

Pilon
Drumstick

Jambon
Ham

Bacon
Bacon

Saucisse
Sausage

Foie
Liver

Faux filet
Sirloin

Les viandes/les poissons/les fruits de mer

Meat/fish/seafood

Filet
Tenderloin

Filet mignon
Filet mignon

Poitrine
Brisket

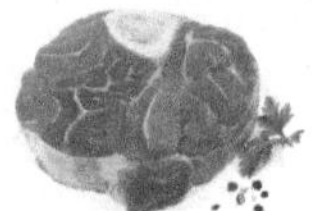

Jarret
Shank

Collier
Chuck

(Sauce au) jus de viande
Gravy

Saignant
Rare

À point
Medium

Bien cuit
Well-done

Œuf
Egg

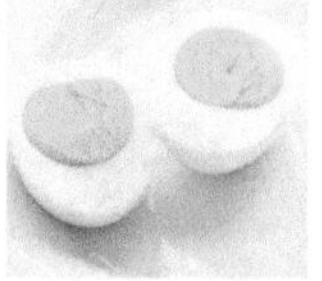

Œufs à la coque
Soft-boiled eggs

Œufs sur le plat
Fried eggs, sunny-side up eggs

Les viandes/les poissons/les fruits de mer

Meat/fish/seafood

 **Œufs durs** Hard-boiled eggs	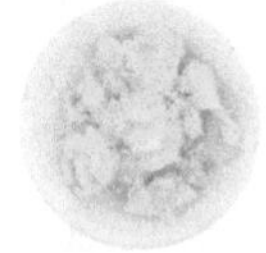 **Œufs brouillés** Scrambled eggs	 **Œufs pochés** Poached eggs
 **Omelette** Omelet		

Phrases clés	Key phrases
Je souhaiterais commander un steak saignant, s'il vous plaît.	I'd like to order a rare steak, please.
À Dimanche, c'est généralement le chef de famille qui découpe le cochon de lait rôti.	On Sundays, the head of the family usually carves the roast suckling pig.
Le poulet est une viande maigre mais l'oie est une viande grasse.	Chicken is a lean meat, but goose is a fatty meat.
Je préfère les œufs brouillés aux œufs sur le plat pour le petit déjeuner.	I prefer scrambled eggs to sunny-side up eggs for breakfast.

Les viandes/les poissons/les fruits de mer

Meat/fish/seafood

Poisson
Fish

Morue, cabillaud
Cod

Saumon
Salmon

Truite
Trout

Sole
Sole

Sardine
Sardine

Thon
Tuna

Bar
Sea bass

Dorade
Sea bream

Flétan
Halibut

Lotte
Monkfish

Colin
Hake

Les viandes/les poissons/les fruits de mer

Meat/fish/seafood

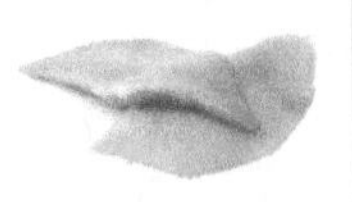

Raie
Ray

Hareng
Herring

Haddock, églefin
Haddock

Maquereau
Mackerel

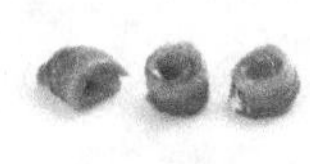

Anchois
Anchovy

Filet de poisson
Fish filet

Arête
Fish bone

Soupe de poisson
Fish soup

Poisson fumé
Smoked fish

Poisson frit
Fried fish

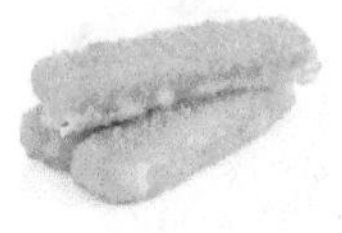

Bâtonnet de poisson
Fish finger, fish stick

Fruits de mer
Seafood

Les viandes/les poissons/les fruits de mer

Meat/fish/seafood

Crabe
Crab

Homard
Lobster

Langouste
Spiny lobster

Tourteau
Rock crab

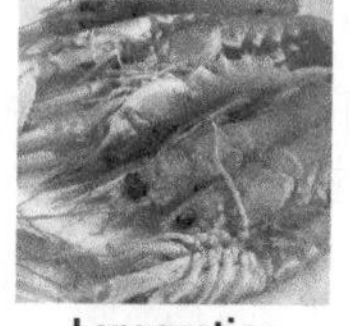

Langoustine
Scampi

Crevettes
Prawn, shrimp

Calamar, encornet
Squid

Poulpe
Octopus

Huître
Oyster

Moule
Mussel

Anguille
Eel

Écrevisse
Crayfish

Les viandes/les poissons/les fruits de mer

Meat/fish/seafood

 **Oursin** Sea urchin	 **Bulot** Whelk	 **Palourde** Clam
 **Coquille Saint-Jacques** Scallop		

Phrases clés	Key phrases
Les coquillages et les crustacés sont meilleurs quand ils sont mangés le jour où ils ont été pêchés.	Shellfish and crustaceans are better when eaten the day they are caught.
Le cabillaud est un poisson maigre mais le saumon est un poisson gras.	Cod is a lean fish, but salmon is an oily fish.
Assure-toi qu'il n'y a plus d'arêtes dans ton poisson avant de le manger.	Make sure there are no bones left in your fish before eating it.

Les légumes
Vegetables

Légume
Vegetable

Haricot vert
Green bean

Haricot rouge
Kidney bean

Haricot noir
Black bean

Fève
Fava bean

Germe de soja
Bean sprout

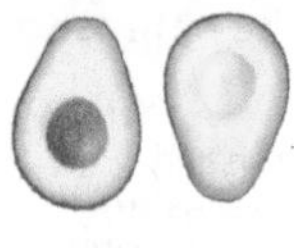

Avocat
Avocado

Maïs
Corn

Tomate
Tomato

Carotte
Carrot

Aubergine
Eggplant, aubergine

Concombre
Cucumber

Les légumes
Vegetables

Courgette
Courgette (UK), zucchini (US)

Brocoli
Broccoli

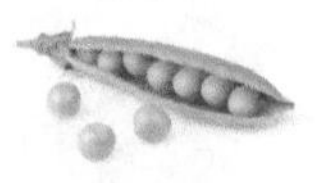

Petit pois
Green pea

Pois chiche
Chickpea

Salade
Salad

Laitue
Lettuce

Roquette
Arugula, rocket

Poireau
Leek

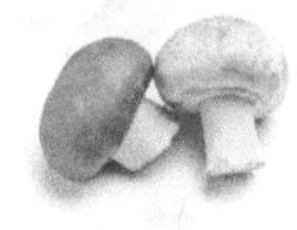

Champignon
Mushroom

Pomme de terre
Potato

Patate douce
Sweet potato

Poivron
Pepper, bell pepper

Les légumes
Vegetables

Chou
Cabbage

Chou-fleur
Cauliflower

Chou de Bruxelles
Brussels sprout

Asperge
Asparagus

Céleri
Celery

Épinards
Spinach

Radis
Radish

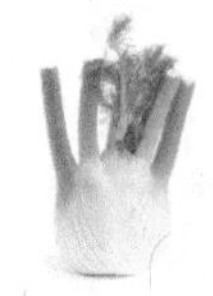

Fenouil
Fennel

Artichaut
Artichoke

Citrouille, potiron
Pumpkin

Courge
Marrow squash

Oignon
Onion

Les légumes
Vegetables

 **Ail** Garlic	 **Échalote** Shallot	 **Panais** Parsnip
 **Navet** Turnip	 **Betterave** Beet, beetroot	

Les légumes
Vegetables

Phrases clés	Key phrases
Est-ce que je peux commander la pizza du chef sans champignons ? Je n'aime pas ça.	Can I order the chef's pizza without mushrooms? I don't like them.
Vos légumes sont-ils bio ?	Are your vegetables organic?
Est-ce que tu vas manger ton gingembre ? Si non, je le prends.	Are you going to eat your ginger? If not, I'll have it.
L'avocat et la tomate sont en réalité des fruits, mais la plupart des gens pensent que ce sont des légumes.	Avocadoes and tomatoes actually are fruits, but most people think they are vegetables.

Les féculents
Starchy foods

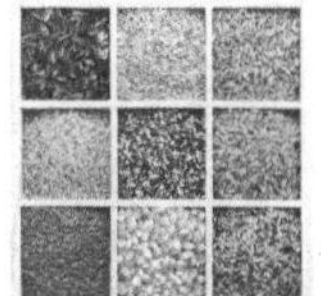 **Céréales** Cereals	 **Légumineuse** Legumes	 **Avoine** Oats
 **Orge** Barley	 **Sarrasin, blé noir** Buckwheat	 **Seigle** Rye
 **Blé** Wheat	 **Épeautre** Spelt	 **Lin** Flax
 **Riz** Rice	 **Riz complet** Brown rice	 **Quinoa** Quinoa

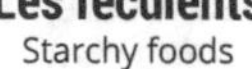

Les féculents
Starchy foods

Lentille
Lentil

Pâtes
Pasta

Nouilles
Noodles

Semoule
Semolina

Phrases clés	Key phrases
Je suis allergique au blé, auriez-vous du pain de seigle ?	I'm allergic to wheat; do you have rye bread?
Est-ce que je peux remplacer les légumes par des frites ?	Can I substitute the vegetables for French fries?
Les céréales, telles que l'avoine, le blé ou l'épautre, sont bonnes pour la santé.	Cereals like oats, wheat or spelt are very healthy.
Parmi les tourtes salées, vous pouvez trouver des tourtes au poulet, des tourtes au lapin voire même des tourtes au steak.	Among savory pies, you can find chicken pies, rabbit pies or even steak pies.

Les desserts
Desserts

Dessert
Dessert

Pâtisserie
Pastry

Tarte
Pie, tart

Farine
Flour

Sucre
Sugar

Glace
Ice cream

Cône de glace
Ice cream cone

Sundae
Sundae

Gâteau
Cake

Chocolat
Chocolate

Pépites de chocolat
Chocolate chips

Bonbons
Sweets, candies

Les desserts
Desserts

Sucette
Lollipop

Tarte aux pommes
Apple pie

Scone
Scone

Gâteau sablé à la crème
Shortcake

Gâteau à la carotte
Carrot cake

Pancake
Pancake

Gâteau au fromage blanc
Cheesecake

Cookies
Cookies

Crème fouettée
Whipped cream

Beignet
Donut

Crème anglaise
Custard

Flan
Custard tart

Les desserts

 **Confiture** Jam	 **Miel** Honey	 **Sirop d'érable** Maple syrup
 **Beurre de cacahuète** Peanut butter	 **Mousse au chocolat** Chocolate mousse	 **Salade de fruits** Fruit salad
 **Pop-corn** Popcorn		

Les desserts
Desserts

Phrases clés	Key phrases
Voulez-vous votre glace dans un pot ou dans un cornet ?	Do you want your ice cream in a cup or in a cone?
Nous avons une sélection de choses que vous pouvez tartiner sur des pancakes : de la confiture, du sirop d'érable ou du beurre de cacahuète.	We have a selection of things you can spread over pancakes: jam, maple syrup or peanut butter.
Quand vous faites de la pâtisserie, vous avez généralement besoin de farine, de sucre et d'œufs.	When baking, you usually need flour, sugar and eggs.
Vous pouvez acheter des bonbons, des sucettes et de la barbe à papa à la fête foraine.	You can buy candies, lollipops and candy floss/ cotton candy at the fairground.

Les fruits
Fruits

 **Fruit** Fruit	 **Pomme** Apple	 **Orange** Orange
 **Clémentine** Tangerine	 **Pêche** Peach	 **Nectarine, brugnon** Nectarine
 **Raisin** Grape	 **Raisin sec** Raisin	 **Ananas** Pineapple
 **Poire** Pear	 **Kiwi** Kiwi, kiwi fruit	 **Figue** Fig

Les fruits
Fruits

Abricot
Apricot

Banane
Banana

Baies, fruits rouges
Berries

Fraise
Strawberry

Mûre
Blackberry

Framboise
Raspberry

Myrtille
Blueberry

Cranberry, canneberge
Cranberry

Groseille
Red currant

Cassis
Black currant

Cerise
Cherry

Pastèque
Watermelon

Les fruits
Fruits

 **Melon** Melon, cantaloupe	 **Pamplemousse** Grapefruit	 **Citron** Lemon
 **Citron vert** Lime	 **Mangue** Mango	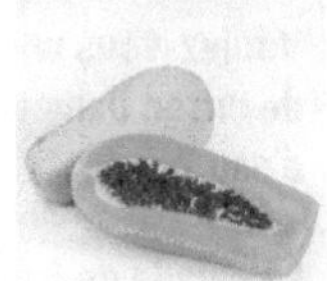 **Papaye** Papaya
 **Noix de coco** Coconut	 **Prune** Plum	 **Datte** Date
 **Fruit de la passion** Passion fruit	 **Grenade** Pomegranate	

Les fruits
Fruits

Phrases clés	Key phrases
Vous pouvez garnir votre yaourt de tranches de banane, de framboises ou de myrtilles.	You can top your yogurt with banana slices, raspberries or blueberries.
Voulez-vous une tranche de citron dans votre verre d'eau ?	Do you want a slice of lemon in your glass of water?
La salade de fruits est composée de pomme, de poire, de kiwi, de banane et de fraise.	The fruit salad is made up of apple, pear, kiwi fruit, banana and strawberry.
Assurez-vous de manger ces fruits avant qu'ils ne pourrissent.	Make sure to eat these fruits before they spoil.
La mangue, la papaye et le fruit de la passion font partie de la famille des fruits tropicaux.	Mango, papaya and passion fruit are part of the tropical fruits family.

Autres types de nourriture
Other types of food

Beurre
Butter

Crème fouettée
Whipped cream

Crème fraîche
Sour cream

Yaourt
Yoghurt, yogurt (US)

Fromage
Cheese

Fromage de chèvre
Goat cheese

Gruyère, emmental
Swiss cheese

Bleu
Blue cheese

Fromage râpé
Grated cheese

Pain
Bread

Pain complet
Whole wheat bread

Pain aux céréales
Multigrain bread

Autres types de nourriture

Other types of food

Pain de maïs
Corn bread

Amande
Almond

Noix
Walnut

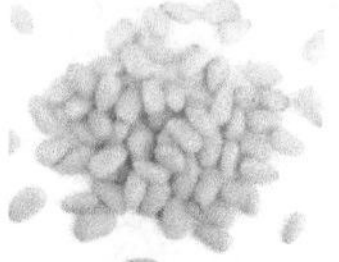

Pignon
Pine nut

Pistache
Pistachio

Noix de cajou
Cashew

Cacahouète
Peanut

Noisette
Hazelnut

Noix de pécan
Pecan

Marron
Chestnut

Noix de macadamia
Macadamla

Graine de potiron
Pumpkin seed

Autres types de nourriture

Other types of food

Graine de moutarde
Mustard seed

Graine de sésame
Sesame seed

Graine de tournesol
Sunflower seed

Graine de lin
Flax seed

Huile d'olive
Olive oil

Huile de sésame
Sesame oil

Huile d'amande
Almond oil

Huile de noix
Walnut oil

Huile de noisette
Hazelnut oil

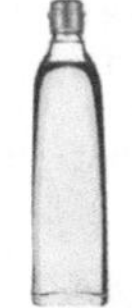

Huile de pépins de raisin
Grapeseed oil

Huile de tournesol
Sunflower oil

Autres types de nourriture

Other types of food

Phrases clés	Key phrases
Notre plateau de fromages est composé d'un mélange de fromages à pâte molle, à pâte semi-molle et à pâte pressée cuite.	Our cheese board is made up of a mix of soft cheese, semi-soft cheese and hard cheese.
Est-ce que je peux remplacer le pain blanc par du pain complet pour mon bagel ?	Can I substitute white bread for multigrain bread for my bagel?
Je suis au régime, donc je dois éviter les plats cuisinés avec de la sauce.	I'm on a diet, so I need to avoid food cooked with cream.
Saupoudrer des graines sur vos salades ou sur certains plats les rend plus sains.	Sprinkling seeds over your salad or some other dishes makes them healthier.
Si vous êtes allergique à certains types de graine ou d'huile, demandez avant de commander votre nourriture.	If you are allergic to some types of seed or oil, always ask before ordering food.

Les assaisonnements/les herbes aromatiques/les épices

Seasoning/herbs/spices

Moutarde
Mustard

Ketchup
Ketchup

Mayonnaise
Mayonnaise, mayo

Vinaigre
Vinegar

Vinaigre balsamique
Balsamic vinegar

Raifort
Horseradish

Sauce pesto
Pesto

Sauce soja
Soy sauce

Sauce pour salade
Salad dressing

Sel
Salt

Poivre
Pepper

Clous de girofle
Dried cloves

Les assaisonnements/les herbes aromatiques/les épices

Seasoning/herbs/spices

Paprika
Paprika

Persil
Parsley

Coriandre
Coriander

Cumin
Cumin

Basilic
Basil

Sauge
Sage

Cannelle
Cinnamon

Bâtons de cannelle
Cinnamon sticks

Aneth
Dill

Muscade
Nutmeg

Laurier sauce
Bay laurel

Bouquet garni
Bouquet garni

Les assaisonnements/les herbes aromatiques/les épices

Seasoning/herbs/spices

Cerfeuil
Chervil

Ciboulette
Chives

Cardamome
Cardamom

Vanille
Vanilla

Curry
Curry

Piment
Chili pepper

Menthe
Mint

Safran
Saffron

Romarin
Rosemary

Origan
Oregano

Curcuma
Turmeric

Thym
Thyme

Les assaisonnements/les herbes aromatiques/les épices

Seasoning/herbs/spices

 **Gingembre** Ginger	 **Fenugrec** Fenugreek	 **Citronnelle** Lemon grass
 **Estragon** Tarragon		

Phrases clés	Key phrases
Je n'aime pas la coriandre, est-ce possible de commander la soupe sans coriandre ?	I don't like coriander; can I order the soup without coriander?
Y a-t-il de la cannelle dans la tarte aux pommes ?	Is there cinnamon in the apple pie?
Voulez-vous du ketchup et de la mayonnaise avec vos frites ?	Do you want ketchup and mayonnaise with your French fries?
Utiliser des herbes et des épices dans une recette peut changer complètement son goût.	Using herbs and spices in a recipe can totally change its taste.

Réserver et passer commande

Making a reservation and ordering

Restaurant
.Restaurant

Restaurant self-service
Self-service restaurant

Fast-food
Fast-food restaurant

Café
Snack-bar, café-restaurant

Salon de thé
Tea shop, tea room

Garçon, serveuse
Waiter, waitress

Menu
Menu

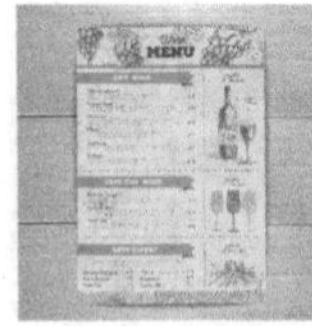

Carte des vins
Wine list

Plat à emporter
Take-out, take-away

Entrées
Starter, appetizer, first course

Plat principal
Main course, entrée (US)

Garniture, accompagnement
Garnish, side

Réserver et passer commande
Making a reservation and ordering

Dessert
Dessert, sweets

Réservation
Reservation

Table
Table

Addition
Bill (UK), check (US)

Pourboire
Tip

Aller au restaurant
To go to the restaurant, to dine out

Faire une réservation
To make a reservation

Commander
To order

Réserver et passer commande

Making a reservation and ordering

Phrases clés	Key phrases
Avez-vous réservé ?	Do you have a reservation?
Désolé, nous sommes complet.	Sorry, we are full.
Nous avons réservé une table pour quatre.	We have reserved a table for four.
Il y a vingt minutes d'attente.	There is a twenty-minute wait.
Bonjour, je m'appelle Jeanne, je serai votre serveuse ce soir.	Hi, my name is Jeanne, I'll be your waitress this evening.
Voulez-vous commencer par un apéritif ?	Would you like to order something to drink first?
Puis-je prendre votre commande ?	May I take your order?
Je vais prendre le poulet avec le riz en accompagnement.	I'll take the chicken with a side of rice.
Je vais commander le crème brûlée.	I'll have the crème brûlée.
Quel assaisonnement voulez-vous pour votre salade ?	What kind of dressing do you want for your salad?
Pouvez-vous amener l'addition, s'il vous plaît ?	Can you bring the bill, please?

Sur la table

On the table

Nappe
Table cloth

Serviette
Napkin

Assiette
Plate

Assiette creuse
Soup dish

Assiette à dessert
Dessert plate

Assiette plate
Dinner plate

Couverts
Cutlery

Cuillère
Tablespoon

Petite cuillère
Teaspoon

Fourchette
Fork

Couteau
Knife

Plat
Serving dish

Sur la table

On the table

Tasse
Cup

Sous-tasse
Saucer

Théière
Teapot

Carafe d'eau
Jug of water

Carafe de vin
Carafe of wine

Carafe à décanter
Decanter

Verre
Glass

Verre à vin
Wine glass

Flûte à champagne
Champagne glass

Bol
Bowl

Saladier
Salad bowl

Sur la table

On the table

Phrases clés	Key phrases
Excusez-moi, pouvez-vous m'apporter une fourchette ? La mienne est tombée par terre.	Excuse me, can you bring me a fork? Mine fell on the floor.
Pouvons-nous avoir une autre bouteille de ce vin ?	Can we have another bottle of this wine?
Sur la table, on trouve généralement une assiette, une fourchette, un couteau, un verre à eau, un verre à vin et une serviette.	On the table, there is usually a plate, a fork, a knife, a water glass, a wine glass and a napkin.
Pour donner un meilleur goût au vin rouge, laissez-le respirer dans une carafe à décanter pendant environ 30 minutes.	To enhance the flavor of a red wine, let it breathe in a decanter for about 30 minutes.

Les spécialités locales

Local specialties

Petit déjeuner
Breakfast

Le croissant
Croissant

La madeleine
Madeleine

Bûche de Noël
Yule log

Pain au chocolat
Chocolate croissant

Steak tartare
Steak tartare

Confit de canard
Duck confit

Brie en Croûte
Baked brie

Gougères
Cheese puffs

Duck à l'Orange
Orange duck

Pot-au-Feu
Stewed beef

Chaussons aux Pommes
Apple Turnovers

Les spécialités locales

Local specialties

Boeuf Bourguignon
Beef Bourguignon

Coq au Vin
Chicken with wine

Cassoulet
Cassoulet

Cordon bleu au poulet
Chicken Cordon Bleu

Quiche Lorraine
Quiche Lorraine

Croque Monsieur
Grilled ham and cheese with Bechamel sauce

Clafoutis aux Cerises
Cherry cobbler

Bouillabaisse
Fish chowder

Ratatouille
Ratatouille

Salade Niçoise
Nicoise salad

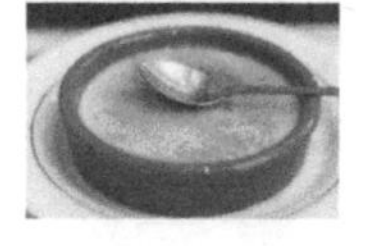

Crème Brûlée
Crème Brûlée

Tarte Tatin
Apple tart

Les spécialités locales
Local specialties

Tartiflette
Scalloped potatoes

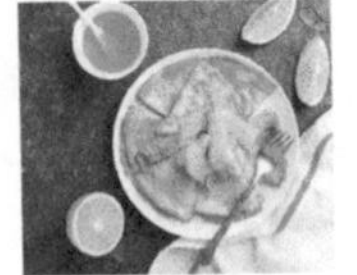

Crêpes Suzette
Crêpes Suzette

Jambon-beurre
Ham sandwich

Steak-frites
Skirt steak and fries

Moules-frites
Mussels and fries

Mousse au Chocolat
Chocolate Mousse

Soufflé au fromage
Cheese Soufflé

Baguette
French bread

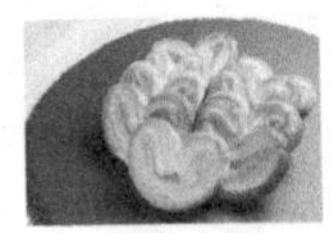

Palmier
Elephant ear

Charcuterie
Sausages and other cured meats

Blanquette de veau
Veal ragout

Beignets
Deep-fried pastry

Les spécialités locales

Local specialties

Escargots
snails

Aligot
Mashed potatoes with cheese

Flamiche
Puff pastry tart made with leeks and cream

Soupe à l'oignon
French onion soup

Les spécialités locales

Local specialties

Phrases clés	Key phrases
Pouvez-vous me dire ce qu'il y a dans le petit déjeuner anglais ?	Can you tell me what's in the English breakfast ?
Quel accompagnement recommandez-vous avec le pain de viande ?	What side do you recommend with the meatloaf?
Les steak-frites et les moulins-frites, les cottage pies et font partie des plats les plus traditionnels de Belgique.	Steak and fries and mussels and fries are some of the most traditional dishes of Belgium.
Le Salade Niçoise sont un plat associé à Provence.	Nicoise salad is a dish associated with Provence.
Les bâtonnets de mozzarella sont souevent mangés en entrée.	Mozzarella sticks are often eaten as an appetizer.

Les menus spécifiques

Special meals

Allergie aux noix
Peanut allergy

Allergie aux fruits à coque
Nut allergy

Allergie aux fruits de mer
Shellfish allergy

Allergie au soja
Soy allergy

Végétarien
Vegetarian

Végan
Vegan

Intolérant au lactose
Lactose intolerant

Sans gluten
Gluten-free

Diabétique
Diabetic

Halal
Halal

Casher
Kosher

Menu enfants
Kids' menu

Les menus spécifiques

Special meals

Phrases clés	Key phrases
Suivez-vous un régime alimentaire spécial ?	Do you have special dietary requirements?
Je suis allergique au homard.	I am allergic to lobster.
Je suis intolérant au lactose donc je ne peux pas manger de fromage.	I'm lactose intolerant, so I can't have cheese.
Avez-vous de la nourriture halal ?	Do you have any halal food?
Une personne lacto-végétarienne boit du lait et mange des produits laitiers, mais ne mange pas de viande, de poisson ou d'œufs.	A lacto-vegetarian person drinks milk and eats dairy goods but doesn't eat meat, fish and eggs.

Sans alcool

Alcohol-free drinks

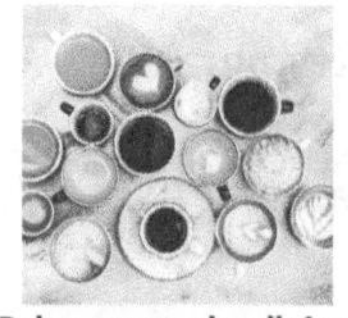

Boissons non alcoolisées
Non-alcoholic drinks

Eau
Water

Eau plate
Still water

Eau pétillante
Sparkling water

Eau du robinet
Tap water

Lait
Milk

Café
Coffee

Thé
Tea

Infusion, tisane
Herbal tea

Chocolat chaud
Hot chocolate

Jus de fruit
Fruit Juice

Jus de légume
Vegetable juice

Sans alcool
Alcohol-free drinks

Jus de pomme
Apple juice

Jus d'orange
Orange juice

Jus d'ananas
Pineapple juice

Jus d'abricot
Apricot juice

Jus de raisin
Grape juice

Jus de tomate
Tomato juice

Jus de carotte
Carrot juice

Limonade
Lemonade

Sirop
Fruit syrup, molasses

Soda
Soft drink

Boisson énergisante
Energy drink

Cocktail sans alcool
Non-alcoholic cocktail

Sans alcool

Alcohol-free drinks

Milkshake Milkshake	**Glaçon** Ice cube

Phrases clés	Key phrases
Voulez-vous de l'eau plate ou eau pétillante ?	Do you want still or sparkling water?
Je vais prendre un jus d'orange.	I'll have an orange juice.
Si vous prenez un soda, vous pouvez remplir votre verre une seconde fois gratuitement.	If you get a soft drink, you can refill your glass for free.
Il y a beaucoup de types de café différents: expresso, flat white, americano, macchiato ...	There are lots of different types of coffee: espresso, flat white, americano, macchiato ...
En France, votre boisson – même l'eau – est servie sans glaçons. Dites « avec glaçons» (« with ice ») si vous en voulez.	In France, your drink – even water – is served without ice. Just say "with ice" if you would like some.

Avec alcool
Alcoholic drinks

Boissons alcoolisées
Alcoholic drinks

Vin rouge
Red wine

Vin blanc
White wine

Vin rosé
Rosé wine

Bouteille
Bottle

Porto
Port

Xérès, sherry
Sherry

Champagne
Champagne

Cidre
Cider

Bière
Beer

Bière à la pression
Draft beer, draught beer, beer on tap

Pinte de bière
Pint of beer

Avec alcool
Alcoholic drinks

Eau-de-vie, cognac
Brandy

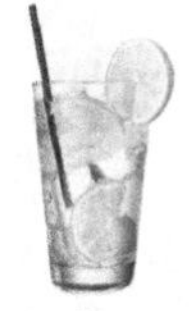

Gin
Gin

Whisky
Whisky, whiskey

Alcool fort
Spirit

Cocktail
Cocktail

Rhum
Rum

Vodka
Vodka

Avec alcool

Alcoholic drinks

Phrases clés	Key phrases
Qu'avez-vous à la pression ?	What do you have on tap?
Je prendrais une pinte, s'il vous plaît.	I'll have a pint, please.
Puis-je voir une pièce d'identité s'il vous plaît ?	Can I see some identification please?
En France, la limite légale d'alcoolémie est de 0.05 %. Cela représente environ deux verres d'alcool.	In France, the legal alcohol limit is 0.05%. This represents about two alcoholic drinks.
En Belgique, la limite légale d'alcoolémie est de 0.05 %.	In Belgium, the legal alcohol limit is 0.05%.

Bonne nuit !

Good night!

L'hôtel

The hotel

Hôtel
Hotel

Appartement hôtel
Extended-stay hotel

Hôtel économique
Budget hotel

Hôtel familial
Family hotel

Hôtel deux étoiles
Two-star hotel

Hôtel cinq étoiles
Five-star hotel

Motel
Motel

Logement
Accommodations

Séjour
Stay

Accueil, réception
Reception, front desk

Date d'arrivée
Arrival date

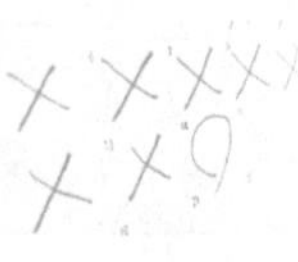

Date de départ
Departure date

L'hôtel

The hotel

Réservation
Booking, reservation

Caution
Deposit

Clé de chambre
Room key

Numéro de chambre
Room number

Facture
Bill

Prix, tarif
Charge

Régler la note
To pay the bill

Laisser un pourboire
To leave a tip

Réclamation
Complaint

Chambres libres
Vacancies

Aucune chambre libre, complet
No vacancies, fully booked

Service de chambre
Room service

L'hôtel

The hotel

Service de blanchisserie
Laundry service

Piscine
Swimming pool

Sauna
Sauna

Jacuzzi
Hot tub

Salle de sport
Gym

Ascenseur
Lift, elevator (US)

Hall
Lobby

Couloir
Corridor, hallway

Étage
Floor

Parking
Car park, parking lot (US)

Sortie de secours
Emergency exit, fire escape

Distributeur automatique
Vending machine

L'hôtel

The hotel

Réveil par téléphone
Wake-up call

Chambre pour une personne
Single room

Chambre pour deux personnes
Double room

Twin beds
Lit jumeaux

Lits superposés
Bunk beds

Chambre pour trois personnes
Triple room

Suite familiale
Family suite

Linge de lit
Linen

Drap
Sheet

Oreiller
Pillow

Couverture
Blanket

Serviette
Towel

L'hôtel

The hotel

Baignoire
Bathtub

Peignoir de bain
Bathrobe

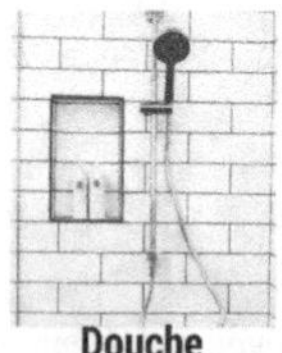

Douche
Shower

Lavabo
Sink

Savon
Soap

Shampoing
Shampoo

Après-shampoing
Conditioner

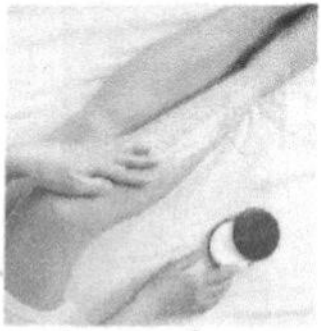

Lotion pour le corps
Body lotion

Mini-bar
Minibar

Air conditionné, climatisation
Air conditioning

Balcon
Balcony

Chambre attenante
Adjoining room

L'hôtel

The hotel

Cintre
Coat hanger

Coffre-fort
Safe

Sèche-cheveux
Hair dryer

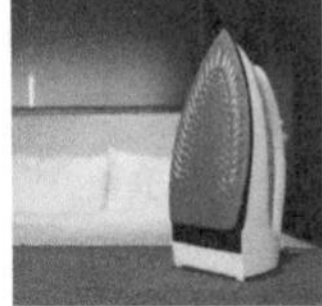

Fer à repasser
Iron

Planche à repasser
Ironing board

Gratuit, offert
Complimentary

Inclus
Included

Client (de l'hôtel)
Guest

Personnel
Staff

Réceptionniste
Receptionist

Femme de chambre
Maid

Concierge
Porter

L'hôtel

The hotel

Gouvernante
Head housekeeper

Femme de ménage
Cleaning lady

Directeur
Manager

S'enregistrer
To check in

Quitter l'établissement
To check out

Réserver
To book

Faire une réservation
To make a reservation

Annuler une réservation
To cancel a reservation

Modifier une réservation
To amend a reservation

L'hôtel

The hotel

Phrases clés	Key phrases
Je cherche un hôtel.	I am looking for a hotel.
Auriez-vous une chambre double libre pour trois nuits.	Do you have a double room available for three nights?
Y a-t-il un autre hôtel près d'ici ?	Is there another hotel nearby?
Combien coûte une nuit d'hôtel ?	How much is the room per night?
À quelle distance se trouve la gare ?	How far is it from the train station?
Y a-t-il du Wi-Fi dans la chambre ?	Is there Wi-Fi in the room?
Je souhaiterais faire une réservation.	I would like to make a reservation.
J'aimerais une chambre double avec une baignoire.	I would like a double room with a bathtub.
Pour combien de nuits ?	For how many nights?

L'hôtel

The hotel

À quelle heure arriverez-vous ?	What time will you arrive?
J'ai fait une réservation au nom de Martin.	I have made a reservation under Martin.
Votre chambre est au troisième étage.	Your room is on the third floor.
À quelle heure doit-on libérer la chambre ?	What time do we have to check out?
Excusez-moi, il y a un problème dans ma chambre.	Excuse me, there's a problem in my room.
Quelles sont les heures d'ouverture de la piscine ?	What are the opening hours of the swimming pool?
Je souhaiterais régler la note.	I would like to check out.
Pouvons-nous laisser nos bagages à l'hôtel après avoir libéré la chambre ?	Can we leave our luggage at the hotel after checking out?

La maison d'hôte et le gîte

The bed and breakfast

Maison d'hôte
Bed and breakfast

Pension de famille
Guest house, boarding house

Hôte, hôtesse
Host, hostess

Pension complète
Full board

Demi-pension
Half board

Petit déjeuner inclus
Breakfast included

Salle de bains attenante, privée
Ensuite bathroom

Salle de bains commune, partagée
Shared bathroom

Salle du petit déjeuner
Breakfast room

Animaux acceptés
Pet-friendly

La maison d'hôte et le gîte

The bed and breakfast

Phrases clés	Key phrases
Y a-t-il un couvre-feu ?	Do you have a curfew?
Votre maison d'hôte accepte-t-elle les animaux ?	Is your bed and breakfast pet-friendly?
Le petit déjeuner est disponible de 7 heures à 9 heures.	Breakfast is from 7am until 9am.
Préférez-vous manger du bacon ou du saumon pour le petit déjeuner ?	Would you rather have bacon or salmon for breakfast?

L'auberge de jeunesse

The youth hostel

Auberge de jeunesse
Youth hostel, hostel

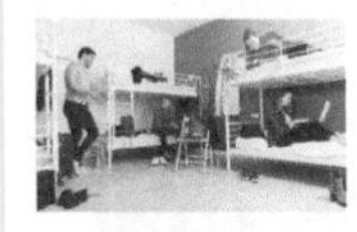

Dortoir
Dorm

Lits superposés
Bunk beds

Lit du haut
Top bunk

Lit du bas
Bottom bunk

Chambre privée
Private room

Bon marché
Cheap

Cuisine
Kitchen

Salle de bains
Bathroom

Buanderie
Laundry room

Machine à laver
Washing machine

Sèche-linge
Dryer

L'auberge de jeunesse

The youth hostel

Casier Locker	**Cadenas** Padlock	**Rideaux** Curtains

Phrases clés	Key phrases
Y a-t-il un lit disponible pour ce soir ?	Is there a bed available for tonight?
Vous avez le choix entre une chambre privée et un dortoir.	You have the choice between a private room or a dorm.
Vous devez utiliser l'échelle pour atteindre le lit du haut.	You need to use the ladder to reach the top bunk.
Si vous voulez un peu plus d'intimité, vous pouvez fermer les rideaux du lit.	If you want some privacy, you can close the bed curtains.
C'est plus sûr de laisser toutes vos affaires dans le casier et de le fermer avec un cadenas.	It is safer to leave all your belongings in the locker and to lock it with a padlock.
N'hésitez pas à utiliser les machines à laver et les sèche-linge dans la buanderie si vous avez besoin de laver vos vêtements.	Feel free to use the washing machines and dryers in the laundry room if you need to wash your clothes.

Le camping
The campground

Campeur
Camper

Emplacement
Location

Terrain de camping
Campsite

Terrain de caravaning
Caravan site

Caravane
Caravan

Mobil-home
Mobile home

Chalet
Chalet

Camping-car
Motor caravan, camper (US)

Tente
Tent

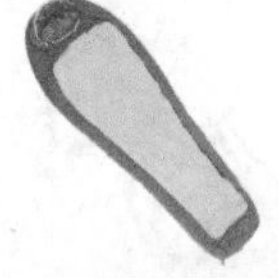

Sac de couchage
Sleeping bag

Matelas pneumatique, matelas gonflable
Air bed, inflatable mattress

Tapis de sol
Ground sheet

Le camping

The campground

Double toit
Fly sheet

Cordage
Rope

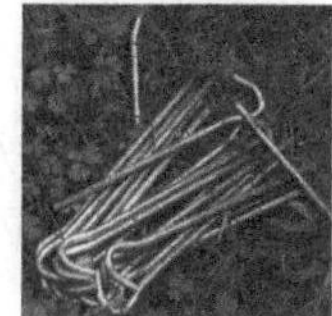

Piquets, sardines
Pegs, hook

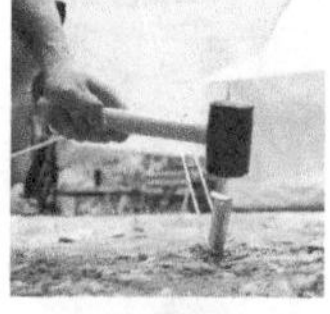

Maillet
Mallet

Sac à dos
Backpack

Lampe de poche, lampe torche
Torch, flashlight

Réchaud, camping-gaz
Stove, camping stove

Recharge de gaz
Gas canister

Gonfleur
Air pump

Gamelle
Billy, billy can, mess kit (US)

Canif
Penknife, pocket knife (US)

Allumettes
Matches, matchsticks

Le camping

The campground

Gourde
Flask

Glacière
Ice cooler

Hammac
Hammock

Siège pliant
Camping chair, folding chair

Table pliante
Folding table

Anti-insectes
Bug spray

Couverture
Rug, blanket

Parasol
Umbrella

Feu de camp
Campfire

Bois de chauffage
Firewood

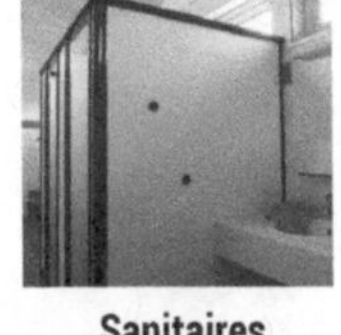

Sanitaires
Toilet block, restrooms

Douches
Showers

Le camping

The campground

Aire de pique-nique
Picnic area

Panier de pique-nique
Picnic basket

Table de pique-nique
Picnic table

Camper
To camp

Planter la tente
To pitch the tent

Démonter la tente
To take down the tent

Faire du caravaning
To go camping (in a tent)

Dormir à la belle étoile
To sleep out in the open

Le camping

The campground

Phrases clés	Key phrases
Où se trouve le terrain de camping ?	Where is the campsite?
Le terrain est-il gardé ?	Is the place guarded?
Vous pouvez choisir un emplacement soit près de la plage soit près des sanitaires.	You can choose a space either near the beach or near the toilet block.
Assurez-vous d'avoir monté votre tente avant la tombée de la nuit parce qu'il fait très sombre.	Make sure you pitch your tent before nightfall, because it gets very dark.
Pour des raisons de sécurité, les feux de camp sont seulement autorisés dans la zone indiquée.	For safety reasons, campfires are only allowed in the designated area.

Séjour chez l'habitant

Homestay

Annonce
Listing

Logement
Accommodations

Maison entière
Entire house

Appartement entier
Entire apartment

Chambre privée
Private room

Chambre partagée
Shared room

Description
Description

Commentaires
Reviews

Emplacement
Location

Hôte, hôtesse
Host

Client, personne
Guest

Chambre
Bedroom

Séjour chez l'habitant

Homestay

Lit
Bed

Équipement
Amenities

Internet sans fil, Wi-Fi
Wireless Internet

Piscine
Pool

Cuisine
Kitchen

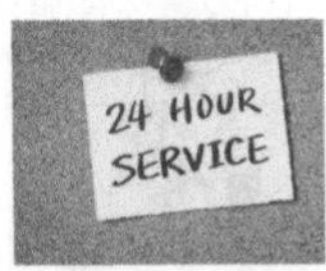

Arrivée possible 24 h/24
24-hour check-in

Air conditionné
Air conditioning

Petit déjeuner
Breakfast

Interphone, interphone sans fil
Buzzer, wireless intercom

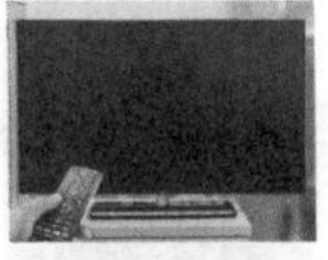

Télévision par cable
Cable TV

Détecteur de monoxyde de carbone
Carbon monoxide detector

Concierge
Doorman

Séjour chez l'habitant

Homestay

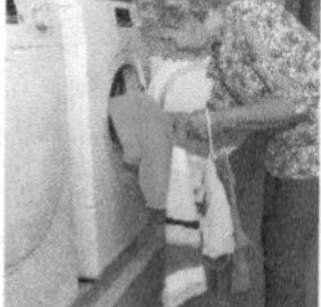

Sèche-linge
Dryer

Ascenseur
Elevator

Produits de base (serviettes, draps, savon, papier toilette, oreillers)
Essentials

Enfants acceptés
Family/kid friendly

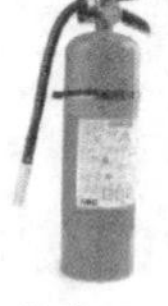

Extincteur
Fire extinguisher

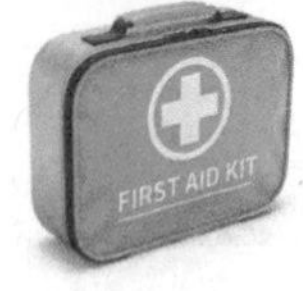

Trousse de secours
First-aid kit

Parking gratuit sur place
Free parking on premises

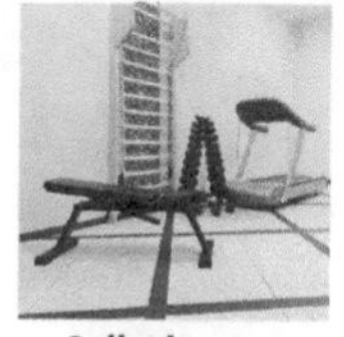

Salle de sport
Gym

Sèche-cheveux
Hair dryer

Cintres
Hangers

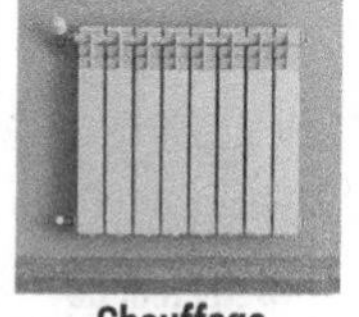

Chauffage
Heating

Jacuzzi
Hot tub

Séjour chez l'habitant

Homestay

Cheminée intérieure
Indoor fireplace

Internet
Internet

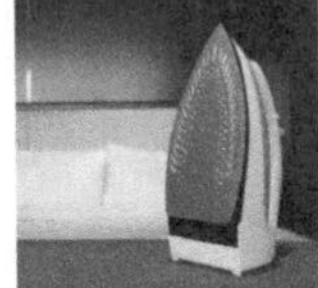

Fer à repasser
Iron

Espace de travail pour ordinateur portable
Laptop-friendly workspace

Serrure sur la porte de la chambre
Lock on bedroom door

Animaux acceptés
Pets allowed

Carte de sécurité
Safety card

Shampoing
Shampoo

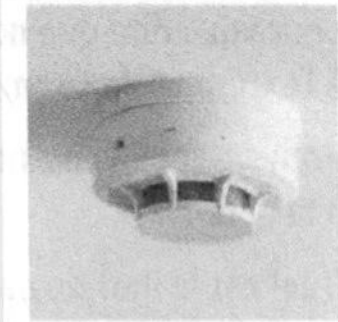

Détecteur de fumée
Smoke detector

Autorisé de fumer
Smoking allowed

Convenable pour des événements
Suitable for events

Télévision
TV

Séjour chez l'habitant

Homestay

Machine à laver
Washer

Accessible aux handicapés
Wheelchair accessible

Phrases clés	Key phrases
Notre vol arrive à 17 heures donc nous devrions être à l'appartement vers 18 h 30.	Our flight arrives at 5pm so we should be at the apartment around 6:30pm.
Comment puis-je vous contacter pour vous dire que nous sommes à l'extérieur de l'immeuble ?	How can I get in touch with you to let you know we are outside the building?
Pouvez-vous venir nous chercher à la gare ?	Can you pick us up at the train station?
Quel est le mot de passe pour le Wi-Fi ?	What's the password for the Wi-Fi?
N'hésitez pas à me solliciter si vous avez besoin de quoi que ce soit.	Don't hesitate to ask if you need anything.
Pouvez-vous recommander un bon restaurant dans les alentours ?	Can you recommend a good restaurant around here?
Où devons-nous laisser les clés à notre départ ?	Where should we leave the keys when we're leaving?

Les types de lit

Types of bed

Lit à une place
Single bed

Lit à deux places
Double bed

Lits jumeaux
Twin beds

Grand lit (152 x 203 cm)
Queen-size bed

Très grand lit (193 x 203 cm)
King-size bed

Très grand lit long (182 x 213 cm)
California king bed

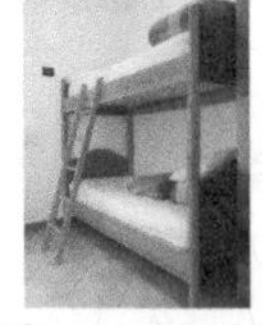

Lits superposés
Bunk beds

Lit à baldaquin
Four-poster bed

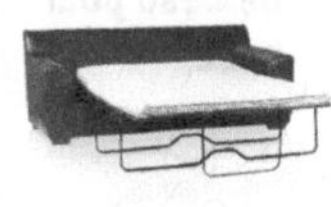

Canapé-lit
Sofa bed

Berceau
Cradle, cot (UK), crib (US)

Futon
Futon

Lit mezzanine
Loft bed

Les types de lit

Types of bed

Phrases clés	Key phrases
Cette chambre a seulement un lit double, mais il y a un canapé-lit pour accueillir une troisième personne.	This room only has one double bed, but there is a sofa bed to accommodate a third person.
Les enfants de moins de 5 ans ne sont pas autorisés à dormir dans les lits mezzanine.	Children under the age of 5 are not allowed to sleep in loft beds.
Si nécessaire, nous pouvons fournir un berceau pour votre bébé.	If needed, we can provide a cradle for your baby.

Les meubles et les équipements

Furniture and amenities

Meubles (pl.)
Furniture

Meuble (sg.)
Piece of furniture

Armoire
Wardrobe

Commode
Chest of drawers, dresser

Tiroir
Drawer

Table de chevet
Nightstand, bedside table

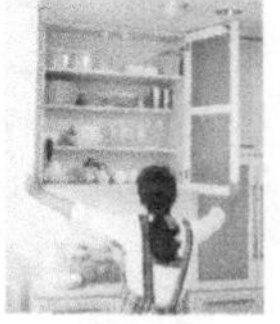

Placard
Cupboard

Bibliothèque
Bookcase

Éclairage
Lighting

Fauteuil
Armchair

Table basse
Coffee table

Bureau
Desk

Les meubles et les équipements

Furniture and amenities

Chaise
Chair

Canapé
Sofa

Porte
Door

Fenêtre
Window

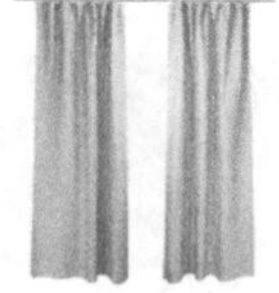

Rideaux
Curtains, drapes

Volet
Shutter

Store
Blinds

Couette
Quilt

Housse de couette
Quilt cover

Couverture
Blanket

Descente de lit
Rug

Dessus-de-lit
Bedspread

Les meubles et les équipements

Furniture and amenities

Drap
Sheet

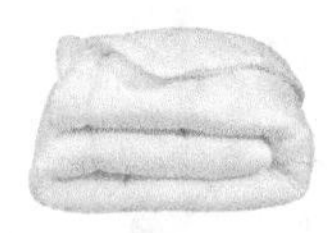

Édredon
Comforter

Literie, linge de lit
Bedding

Oreiller
Pillow

Taie d'oreiller
Pillowcase

Tapis
Carpet, rug

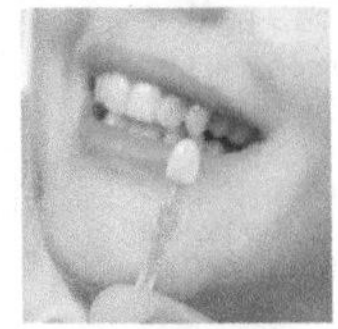

Télécommande
Remote control

Lampe
Lamp

Lampe de chevet
Bedside lamp

Lampe de bureau
Desk lamp

Abat-jour
Lampshade

Ampoule
Light bulb

Les meubles et les équipements

Furniture and amenities

Réveil
Alarm clock

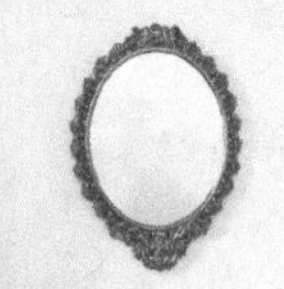

Miroir
Mirror

Phrases clés	Key phrases
Il a y un problème avec ma chambre, la porte ne veut pas s'ouvrir.	There is a problem with my room; the door won't open.
Pouvez-vous m'indiquer comment utiliser la télécommande s'il vous plaît ?	Can you tell me how to use the remote control, please?
Excusez-moi, est-il possible d'avoir un oreiller supplémentaire ?	Excuse me, is it possible to have an extra pillow?
La lampe de chevet ne fonctionne pas, je crois que l'ampoule a grillé.	The bedside lamp is not working; I think the light bulb burned out.
Pourriez-vous changer les draps dans ma chambre aujourd'hui, s'il vous plaît ?	Could you please change the bedsheets in my room today?

Le bain/la douche

The bath/the shower

Meuble de salle de bains
Bathroom cabinet

Robinet
Tap, faucet (US)

Lavabo
Washbasin, bathroom sink

Baignoire
Bathtub

Trou d'écoulement
Plughole, drain (US)

Bonde
Plug

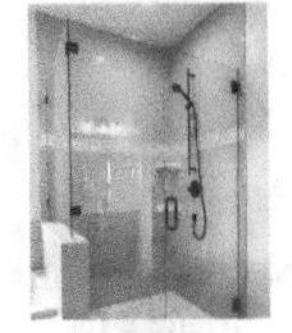

Douche
Shower

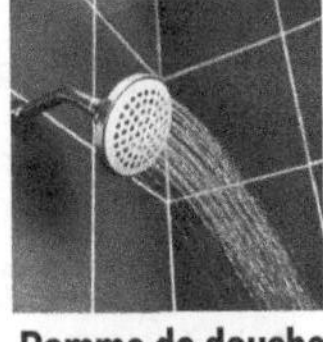

Pomme de douche
Showerhead

Plafonnier de douche
Rain shower head

Tapis de bain
Bath mat

Savon
Soap

Gel douche
Shower gel

Le bain/la douche

The bath/the shower

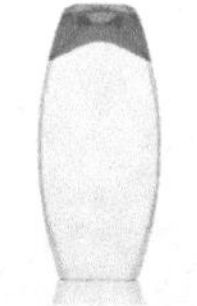 **Shampoing** Shampoo	 **Après-shampoing** Conditioner	 **Serviette** Towel
 **Gant de toilette** Washcloth	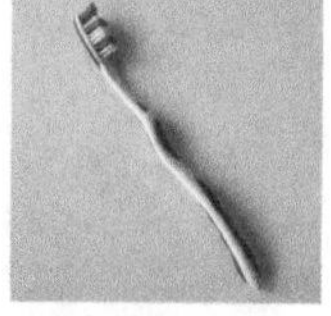 **Brosse à dents** Toothbrush	 **Porte-brosse à dents** Toothbrush holder
 **Dentifrice** Toothpaste	 **Bain de bouche** Mouthwash	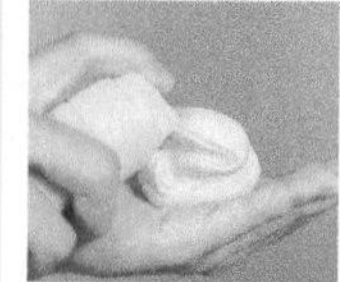 **Crème à raser, mousse à raser** Shaving cream, shaving foam
 **Rasoir** Razor	 **Rasoir électrique** Electric razor	 **Après-rasage** Aftershave

Le bain/la douche

The bath/the shower

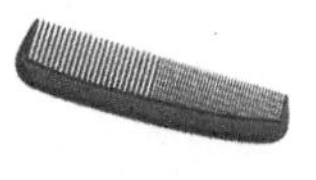

Peigne
Comb

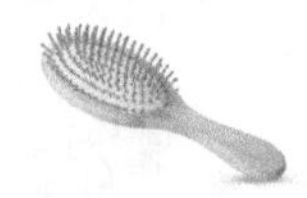

Brosse
Hair brush

Chouchou
Scrunchie

Sèche-cheveux
Hair dryer

Maquillage
Makeup, cosmetics

Parfum
Perfume

Coton-tige
Cotton swab

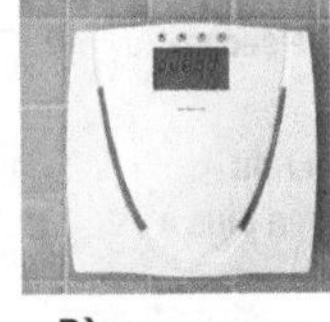

Pèse-personne
Scale

Prendre un bain
To take a bath

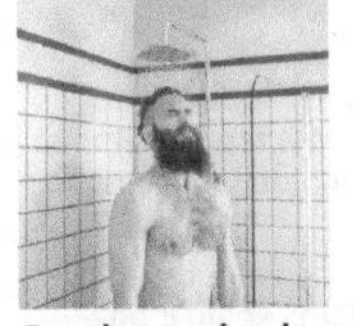

Prendre une douche
To take a shower

Se sécher
To dry oneself

Se brosser les dents
To brush one's teeth

Le bain/la douche

The bath/the shower

Se peigner les cheveux
To comb one's hair

(Se) Raser
To shave

Phrases clés	Key phrases
L'hôtel fournit un kit d'articles de toilette qui contient tout ce dont vous avez besoin pour deux jours.	The hotel provides a toiletries kit that contains everything you need for a couple of days.
Vous aurez peut-être besoin d'un transformateur pour utiliser votre rasoir électrique ou votre sèche-cheveux à l'étranger.	You might need a power converter to use your electric razor or your hair dryer abroad.
N'hésitez pas à demander du savon ou du shampoing en plus à la femme de chambre.	Feel free to ask the maid for extra soap or shampoo.
Pouvez-vous changer les serviettes dans la salle de bains s'il vous plaît ?	Could you change the towels in the bathroom, please?
Serait-il possible d'avoir plus de shampoing et d'après-shampoing s'il vous plaît ?	Would it be possible to have some more shampoo and conditioner, please?
Il n'y a pas de sèche-cheveux dans notre chambre, serait-il possible d'en avoir un ?	There is no hair dryer in our room; would it be possible to have one?

Les toilettes

The toilets

Toilettes, W.C.
Toilet, bathroom

Toilettes pour femmes
Ladies' room

Toilettes pour hommes
Men's room

Toilettes (informel)
Loo, john

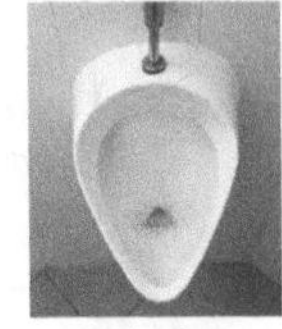

Urinoire
Urinal

Papier toilette
Toilet paper

Lavabo
Washbasin, bathroom sink

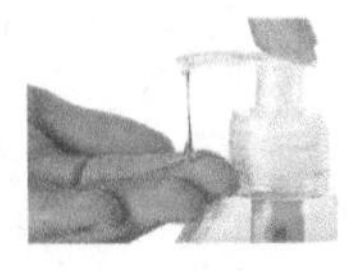

Savon pour les mains
Hand soap

Sèche-mains
Hand dryer

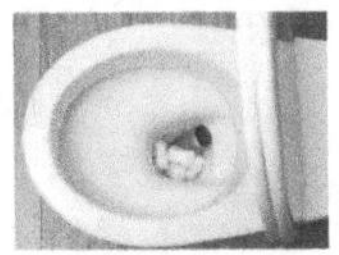

Bouché
Clogged

Ventouse
Plunger

Désodorisant pour toilettes
Bathroom air freshener

Les toilettes

The toilets

Phrases clés	Key phrases
Excusez-moi, où sont les toilettes ?	Excuse me, where is the bathroom?
Pourriez-vous m'indiquer les toilettes pour femmes ?	Could you direct me to the ladies' room?
Excusez-moi, les toilettes de notre chambre sont bouchées.	Excuse me, the toilet in our room is clogged.

Les sorties

Let's go out!

Combien ça coûte ?

How much is it?

Zéro
Zero, nought

Un
One

Deux
Two

Trois
Three

Quatre
Four

Cinq
Five

Six
Six

Sept
Seven

Huit
Eight

Neuf
Nine

Dix
Ten

Onze
Eleven

Combien ça coûte ?

How much is it?

Douze
Twelve

Treize
Thirteen

Quatorze
Fourteen

Quinze
Fifteen

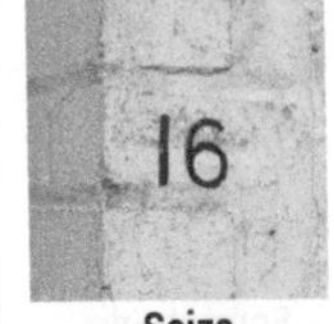

Seize
Sixteen

Dix-sept
Seventeen

Dix-huit
Eighteen

Dix-neuf
Nineteen

Vingt
Twenty

Vingt et un
Twenty-one

Vingt-deux
Twenty-two

Vingt-cinq
Twenty-five

Combien ça coûte ?

How much is it?

Trente
Thirty

Quarante
Forty

Cinquante
Fifty

Soixante
Sixty

Soixante-dix
Seventy

Quatre-vingts
Eighty

Quatre-vingt-dix
Ninety

Cent
One hundred

Deux cents
Two hundred

Cinq cent soixante-deux
Five hundred sixty-two

Mille
One thousand

Deux mille
Two thousand

Combien ça coûte ?

How much is it?

1000000

Un million
One million

2,000,000

Deux millions
Two million

Un milliard
One billion

Deux milliards
Two billion

Prix
Price

Prix de vente
Selling price

Étiquette
Price tag

Bon marché
Cheap

Cher
Expensive

À prix réduit
Reduced

À moitié prix
Half price

Soldes
Sales

Combien ça coûte ?

How much is it?

TVA (Taxe sur la Valeur Ajoutée)
VAT (Value Added Tax)

Total
Total

Monnaie
Change

Acheter
To buy, to purchase

Vendre
To sell

Dépenser
To spend

Payer
To pay

Combien ça coûte ?

How much is it?

Phrases clés	Key phrases
Combien ça coûte ?	How much does it cost?
Excusez-moi, combien coûte cette paire de chaussures ?	Excuse me, how much is this pair of shoes?
Ça coûte quarante-neuf euros (€ 49).	It costs forty-nine euros (€49).
C'est trop cher, avez-vous quelque chose de moins cher ?	It's too expensive; do you have something cheaper?
J'adorerais pouvoir acheter cette veste mais je n'en ai pas les moyens.	I would love to buy this jacket, but I can't afford it.
Je vais payer avec une carte de crédit.	I'll pay by credit card.
Je vais payer en espèces.	I'll pay with cash.

La monnaie/les billets/la carte bleue/le distributeur automatique

Coins/notes/bank card/ATM

Pièce de monnaie
Coin

Billet
Note, bill (US)

Pièce de dix cents
Ten-pence coin

Pièce de cinquante cents
Fifty-cent coin

Pièce d'une euro
One-euro coin

Pièce de deux euro
Two-euro coin

Billet de cinq euro
Five-euro note

La monnaie/les billets/la carte bleue/le distributeur automatique

Coins/notes/bank card/ATM

Billet de dix euro

Ten-euro note

Billet de vingt euro

Twenty-euro note

Billet de cinquante euro

Fifty-euro note

La monnaie/les billets/la carte bleue/le distributeur automatique

Coins/notes/bank card/ATM

Banque
Bank

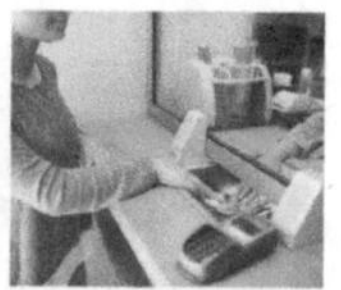

Bureau de change
Currency exchange office

Carte bancaire
Bank card, ATM card (US)

Carte de crédit
Credit card

PIN, code secret
PIN, secret code

Devise, monnaie
Currency

Devise étrangère
Foreign currency

Chèque
Cheque, check

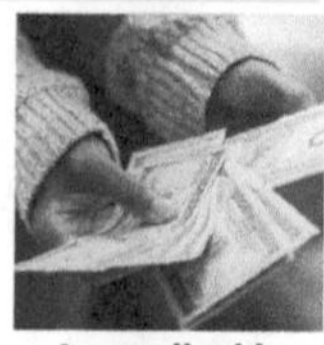

Argent liquide
Cash

Chèque de voyage
Traveller's cheque (UK), traveler's check (US)

La monnaie/les billets/la carte bleue/le distributeur automatique

Coins/notes/bank card/ATM

Taux de change
Exchange rate

Virement bancaire
Bank transfer

Employé de banque
Bank clerk/teller

Directrice de banque
Bank manager

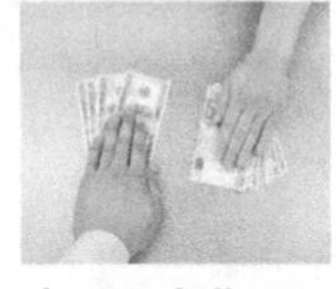

Changer de l'argent (en euros)
To change money (into euros)

Payer en espèces
To pay with cash

Retirer
To withdraw

Distributeur automatique
ATM, cash dispenser

Compte courant
Current account (UK), checking account (US)

Compte épargne
Savings account

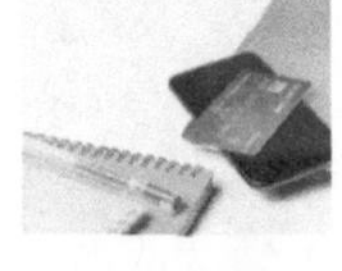

Compte crédit
Credit account

Compte à découvert
Overdrawn account

La monnaie/les billets/la carte bleue/le distributeur automatique

Coins/notes/bank card/ATM

Retrait
Withdrawal

Dépôt
Deposit

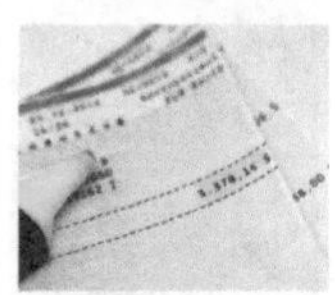

Solde du compte
Account balance

Virement/règlement bancaire
Transfer/electronic payment

Reçu
Receipt

Écran
Screen

Touches de l'écran
Screen buttons

Clavier
Keypad

Distributeur de reçus
Receipt dispenser

Lecteur de carte
Card reader

La monnaie/les billets/la carte bleue/le distributeur automatique

Coins/notes/bank card/ATM

Phrases clés	Key phrases
Où puis-je changer de l'argent ?	Where can I exchange money?
Où puis-je trouver une banque ?	Where can I find a bank?
Changez-vous des devises étrangères ici ?	Do you change foreign currency here?
Quel est le taux de change aujourd'hui ?	What is the exchange rate today?
Prenez-vous une commission ?	Do you charge a fee?
J'aimerais changer de l'argent s'il vous plaît.	I'd like to exchange money, please.
J'aimerais changer des chèques de voyage.	I'd like to change some traveler's checks.
Veuillez insérer votre carte.	Please insert your card.
Entrez votre PIN (code secret) puis appuyez sur « Enter ».	Enter your PIN and then press "Enter."

La monnaie/les billets/la carte bleue/le distributeur automatique

Coins/notes/bank card/ATM

Choisissez le type de transaction que vous voulez réaliser.	Choose the type of transaction you want to make.
Vous avez demandé 100 Euros Est-ce correct ?	You've asked for €100.00 Is that correct?
Votre demande est en cours de traitement.	Your request is being processed.
Veuillez retirer votre argent.	Please remove your cash.
Souhaitez-vous réaliser une autre transaction ?	Would you like to make another transaction?
Veuillez retirer votre carte et prendre votre reçu.	Please remove your credit card and take your receipt.

Les boutiques

The shops

Magasin
Shop, store (US)

Petit commerçant
Shopkeeper

Marché
Market

Étal, éventaire
Stall

Grand magasin
Department store

Rayon
Department

Galerie commerciale
Shopping mall, arcade

Zone piétonne commerçante
Pedestrian mall

Employé
Shop assistant, salesman, sales clerk (US)

Client
Customer

Vitrine
Shop window

Voleur à l'étalage
Shoplifter

Les boutiques

The shops

Boulangerie
Bakery

Pâtisserie
Pastry shop

Boulanger, boulangère
Baker

Boucherie
Butcher's

Boucher, bouchère
Butcher

Poissonerie
Fishmonger's

Poissonier, poissonière
Fishmonger

Épicerie fine
Delicatessen

Salon de coiffure
Hairdresser's salon/shop

Coiffeur, coiffeuse
Hairdresser

Coiffeur pour hommes
Barber

Fleuriste (magasin)
Flower shop

Les boutiques

The shops

Fleuriste (personne)
Florist

Pharmacie
Pharmacy, drugstore

Pharmacien, pharmacienne
Pharmacist

Parfumerie
Perfume shop

Magasin de vêtements
Clothes shop

Magasin de chaussures
Shoe shop

Librairie
Bookstore

Libraire
Bookseller

Papeterie
Stationery shop

Marchand de journaux
Newsagent's, newstand (US)

Bureau de poste
Post office

Salon de beauté
Beauty salon

Les boutiques

The shops

Quincaillerie
Hardware store

Animalerie
Pet store

Laverie automatique
Laundromat, launderette

Pressing
Dry cleaner's

Cordonnerie
Shoe repair

Magasin de confiseries
Confectionery, sweet shop, candy shop

Magasin de vins et liqueurs
Wine shop, liquor store

Bijouterie
Jeweler's

Bijoutier, bijoutière
Jeweler

Boutique de cadeaux
Gift shop

Caisse
Cash desk (UK), checkout counter (US)

Bonne affaire
Bargain

Les boutiques

The shops

Faire les magasins
To go shopping

Faire du lèche-vitrine
To go window-shopping

Phrases clés	Key phrases
Je souhaiterais acheter quelques souvenirs.	I would like to buy some souvenirs.
Acceptez-vous les cartes de crédit ?	Do you accept credit cards?
Y a-t-il une boulangerie dans les alentours ?	Is there a bakery around here?
Tu peux acheter des timbres au bureau de poste.	You can buy stamps at the post office.
Ces chaussures étaient une bonne affaire.	These shoes were a bargain.

Le supermarché

The supermarket

Supermarché
Supermarket

Magasin d'alimentation
Grocery store

Magasin de quartier
Convenience store

Allée, rayon
Aisle

Étagère
Shelf

Chariot
Trolley (UK),
Shopping cart (US)

Panier
Basket

Produits agricoles
Produce

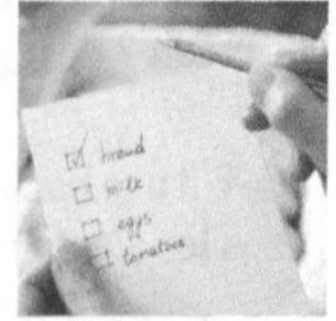

Liste de courses
Shopping list

Marchandises
Goods

Article
Item

Offre spéciale
Special offer

Le supermarché

The supermarket

Remise
Discount

Caisse
Checkout counter

Caissier, caissière
Cashier, checkout assistant

File d'attente à la caisse
Checkout line

Caisse enregistreuse
Cash register

Code-barres
Barcode

Caisse libre-service
Self-checkout

Sac plastique/en papier
Plastic/paper bag

Le supermarché

The supermarket

Phrases clés	Key phrases
Où puis-je trouver le lait ?	Where can I find the milk?
Où sont les céréales pour le petit déjeuner ?	Where are the breakfast cereals?
Vendez-vous du pain pita ?	Do you sell pita bread?
Avez-vous besoin d'un sac ?	Do you need a bag?

Les cadeaux

Gifts

Cadeau
Gift, present

Cadeau d'anniversaire
Birthday present

Cadeau de Noël
Christmas present

Cadeau de mariage
Wedding present

Carte cadeau
Gift card

Emballage
Wrapping

Papier cadeau
Wrapping paper

Bolduc
Curling ribbon, gift-wrap ribbon

Faire un paquet-cadeau
To gift wrap a package

Les cadeaux

Gifts

Phrases clés	Key phrases
Je t'ai acheté un petit quelque chose.	I got you a little something.
Ce n'est pas grand-chose mais j'espère que ça te plaira.	It's just something small, but I hope you like it.
C'est pour toi, j'ai pensé que ce serait parfait pour ta nouvelle maison.	This is for you; I thought it would be perfect for your new home.
C'est pour ta pendaison de crémaillère.	This is for your housewarming party.
C'est si gentil de ta part !	It is so nice of you!
Tu n'avais pas besoin de faire ça !	You didn't have to do that!
Quelle délicate attention, merci beaucoup !	That's so thoughtful of you; thank you so much!

L'artisanat

Handicrafts

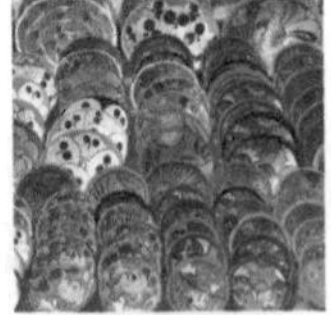

Artisanat
Craftwork, handicraft (US)

Savoir-faire artisanal
Craftsmanship

Artisan
Artisan, craftsman, craftswoman

Compagnon
Journeyman

Compétences
Skills

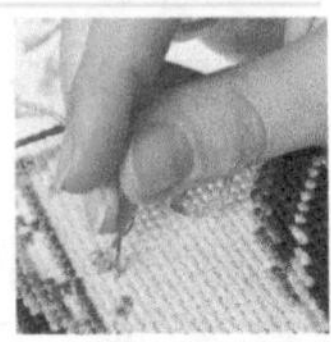

Travaux d'aiguille
Needlework

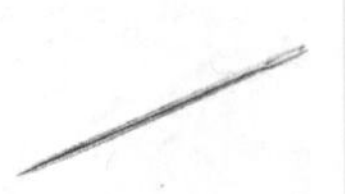

Aiguille
Needle

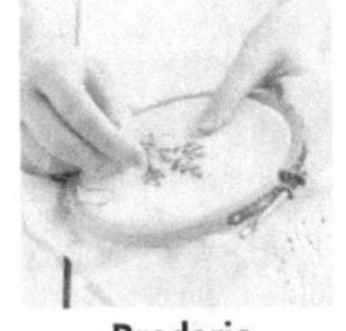

Broderie
Embroidery

Métier à broder
Embroidery hoop

Aquarelle
Watercolour/watercolor

Argenterie
Silverware

Argile
Clay

Le shopping

L'artisanat

Handicrafts

Atelier
Workshop, studio

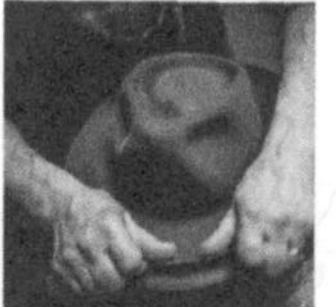

Chapelier
Hatter

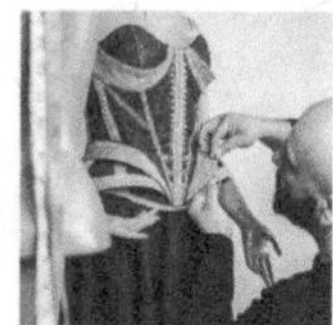

Costume
Costume, dress

Couture
Dressmaking

Couturier, couturière
Dressmaker

Tailleur
Tailor

Modiste
Milliner

Tapisserie
Tapestry

Tapisserie d'ameublement
Upholstery

Tissage
Weaving

Tisserand
Weaver

Forgeron
Blacksmith

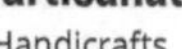

L'artisanat
Handicrafts

Forge
Smithy

Guilde, corporation, confrérie
Guild

Apothicaire
Apothecary

Coutelier
Cutler (knife maker)

Orfèvre
Goldsmith, silversmith

Maçonnerie
Stonework

Maçon
Mason

Menuiserie
Carpentry, woodwork, joinery

Menuisier
Woodworker, joiner

Poterie
Pottery

Potier
Potter

Tour de potier
Potter's wheel

L'artisanat
Handicrafts

Ouvrier verrier
Glassworker

Artiste verrier
Glass artist

Vitrier
Glazier

Phrases clés	Key phrases
Ce village est connu pour son artisanat.	This village is known for its craftwork.
J'adorerais visiter une poterie.	I would love to visit a pottery.
J'aurais aimé être une couturière, mais je n'ai pas les compétences.	I would have liked to be a dressmaker, but I don't have the skills.

Les vêtements

Clothes

Vêtements
Clothes

Vêtement
Article of clothing

Sous-vêtement
Underwear

Tissu
Material, fabric

Prêt-à-porter
Ready-to-wear

Mode
Fashion

Laine
Wool

Coton
Cotton

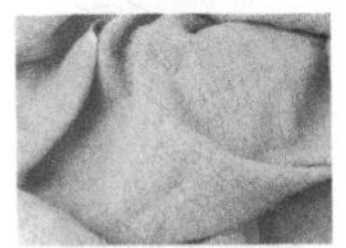

Lin
Linen

Soie
Silk

Velours
Velvet

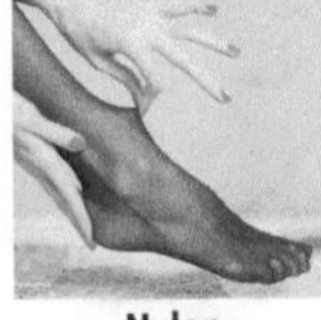

Nylon
Nylon

Les vêtements

Clothes

Cuir
Leather

Fourrure
Fur

Uniforme
Uniform

Caleçon
Boxer shorts

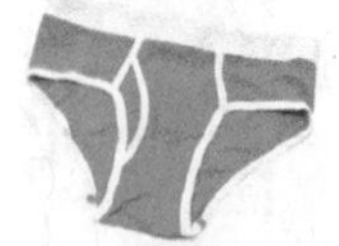

Slip
Briefs

Slip de bain
Swimming trunks (Speedos)

Maillot de bain
Swimsuit

Chemise
Shirt

Col
Collar

Manche
Sleeve

Poignets, manchettes
Cuffs

Pantalon
Trousers, pants

Les vêtements

Clothes

Jean
Jeans

Pli
Crease

Short
Shorts

Veste
Jacket

Manteau
Coat

Pardessus
Overcoat

Imperméable
Raincoat

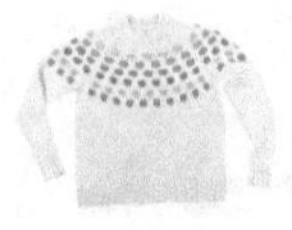

Pull-over
Pullover, sweater

Gilet
Waistcoat, vest

Poche
Pocket

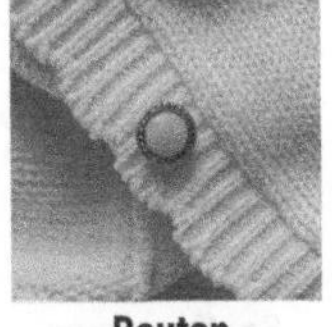

Bouton
Button

Doublure
Lining

Les vêtements

Clothes

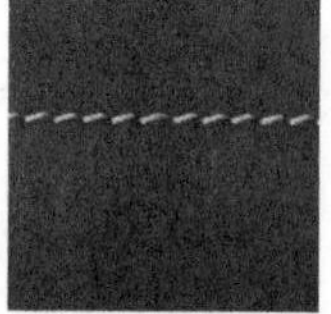

Couture
Seam

Smoking
Dinner-jacket, tuxedo

Pyjama
Pyjamas, pajamas (US)

Blazer
Blazer

Salopette
Overalls, coveralls (US)

Survêtement
Tracksuit, sweatpants

Tee shirt
T-shirt

Pull à capuche
Hoodie

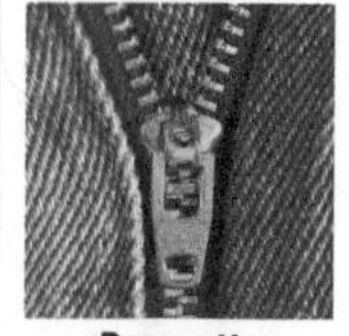

Braguette
Fly

Polo
Polo shirt

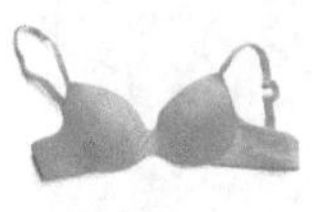

Soutien-gorge
Bra

Gaine
Girdle

Les vêtements

Clothes

Culotte, slip
Panties, briefs

Bas
Stockings

Collants
Tights

Jupe
Skirt

Corsage, chemisier
Blouse

Pull-over
Jumper (UK), sweater (US)

Robe
Dress

Tailleur
Suit

Robe
Gown

Capuche
Hood

À la mode, élégant
Fashionable

Démodé
Old-fashioned

Les vêtements

Clothes

De bon goût
Tasteful

De mauvais goût
Tasteless

Élégant, chic
Elegant, smart

Lâche, ample
Loose, baggy

Étroit, serré
Tight, close-fitting

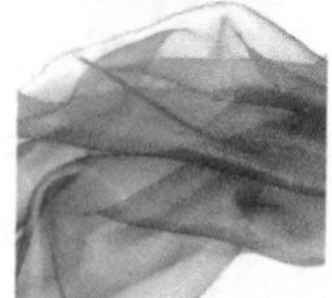

Léger
Light

Lourd
Heavy

Gros, grossier
Coarse

Fin
Fine

Laineux
Wooly

Soyeux
Silky

Mou
Soft

Les vêtements

Clothes

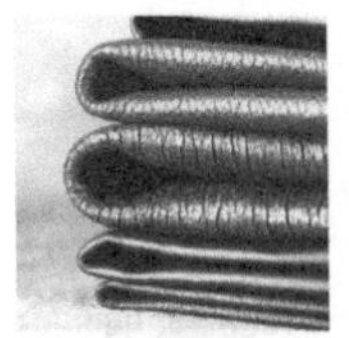

Dur, rigide
Stiff

S'habiller
To dress

Porter
To wear

Mettre un vêtement
To put on a garment

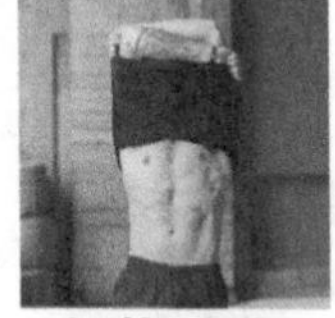

Se déshabiller
To undress

Enlever, ôter
To take off

Se mettre sur son trente-et-un
To put on one's Sunday best

Aller, être à la bonne taille
To fit

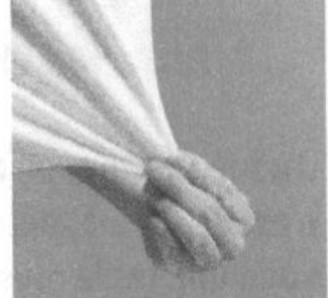

S'allonger, s'élargir
To stretch

Rétrécir
To shrink

Teindre
To dye

Nouer
To tie

Les vêtements

The clothes

Plier
To fold

S'habiller avec élégance
To dress up

Boutonner quelque chose
To button something up

Déboutonner
To unbutton something

Fermer la fermeture éclair
To zip something up

Ouvrir la fermeture éclair
To unzip

Phrases clés	Key phrases
J'adore cette robe mais elle n'est pas à ma taille. Avez-vous une taille plus petite ?	I love this dress, but it doesn't fit me. Do you have a smaller size?
C'est un tailleur très élégant.	This is a very smart suit.
J'ai dû déboutonner mon pantalon après le déjeuner parce que j'ai trop mangé.	I've had to unbutton my pants after lunch because I ate too much.
J'ai oublié de prendre un maillot de bain.	I forgot to pack a swimsuit.
La braguette de mon jean vient de se casser !	The fly of my jeans just broke!

Les chaussures
Shoes

Chaussures
Shoes

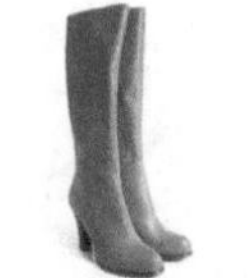

Bottes, chaussures montantes
Boots

Bottes en caoutchouc
Rubber boots

Bottines
Booties

Baskets, chaussures de sport
Sneakers, trainers, running shoes

Chaussures de randonnée
Hiking boots

Chaussons
Slippers

Escarpins
Court/pump shoes

Chaussures à talon haut
High heel shoes

Mocassins
Loafers

Sabots
Clogs

Sandales
Sandals

Les chaussures

Shoes

Talons aiguilles
Stilettos

Tong, savate
Flip-flops

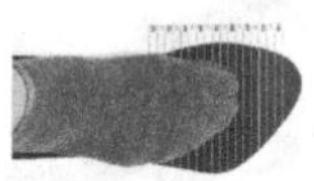

Pointure
Size

Cuir
Leather

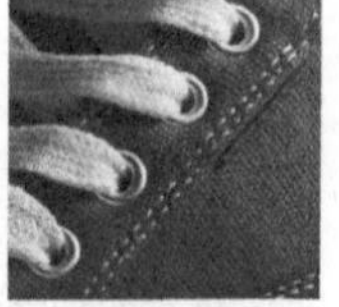

Toile
Canvas

Lacets
Laces, shoelaces

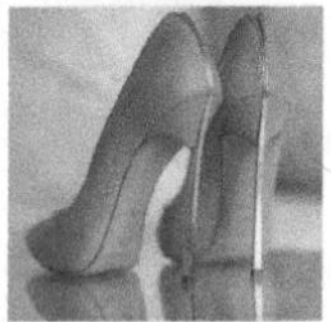

Talon
Heel

Semelle
Sole

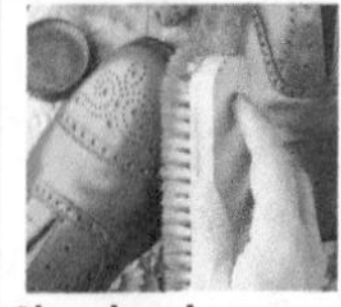

Cirer des chaussures
To black, to polish, to shine shoes

Lacer
To lace up

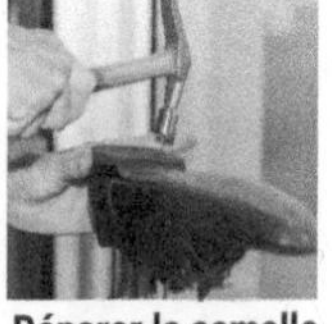

Réparer la semelle
To mend the sole

Ressemeler
To resole

Les chaussures

Shoes

Phrases clés	Key phrases
Quelle pointure faites-vous ?	What is your shoe size?
Vous pouvez retirer vos chaussures.	You can take off your shoes.
Mets tes chaussons !	Put on your slippers!
Pouvez-vous réparer la semelle de mes chaussures ?	Can you mend the sole of my shoes?
Mes lacets ont cassé, est-ce que vous en vendez ?	My shoelaces broke; do you sell them?

Les accessoires

Accessories

Ceinture
Belt

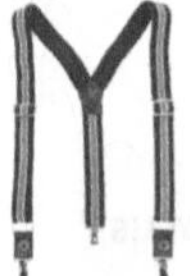

Bretelles
Braces, suspenders

Boucle de ceinture
Buckle

Chapeau melon
Bowler

Chapeau de feutre
Felt hat

Haut de forme
Top hat

Chapeau à bord large
Broad-brimmed hat

Casquette
Cap

Chapeau
Hat

Bandeau
Headband

Écharpe
Scarf

Gants
Gloves

Les accessoires

Accessories

Moufles
Mittens

Cravate
Tie

Nœud papillon
Bow-tie

Parapluie
Umbrella

Portefeuille
Wallet

Sac à main
Handbag

Mouchoir
Handkerchief

Mouchoir en papier
Tissue

Bijoux
Jewelry

Alliance
Wedding ring

Bague
Ring

Boucle d'oreille
Earring

Les accessoires
Accessories

Boutons de manchette
Cufflinks

Bracelet
Bracelet

Broche
Brooch

Collier
Necklace

Diamant
Diamond

Montre
Watch

Perle
Pearl

Les accessoires

Accessories

Phrases clés	Key phrases
Le temps est plus froid que prévu, il faut que j'achète une écharpe et des gants.	The weather is colder than expected; I have to buy a scarf and gloves.
Peux-tu m'aider à nouer ma cravate ?	Can you help tie my tie?
N'oublie pas de prendre un parapluie, il est censé pleuvoir aujourd'hui.	Don't forget to take an umbrella; it's supposed to rain today.
Pouvez-vous nous montrer les alliances ?	Can you show us the wedding rings?

En plein air

Outdoor sports

Football
Football (UK), soccer (US)

Tennis
Tennis

Basket-ball
Basketball

Base-ball
Baseball

Handball
Handball

Volley-ball
Volleyball

Cricket
Cricket

Rugby
Rugby

Équitation
Horse riding

Polo
Polo

Golf
Golf

Cyclisme
Cycling

En plein air
Outdoor sports

Marche
Walking

Randonnée
Hiking

Escalade
Climbing

Tir à l'arc
Archery

Athlétisme
Athletics, track and field

110 mètres haies
110 m hurdles

Triathlon
Triathlon

Décathlon
Decathlon

Heptathlon
Heptathlon

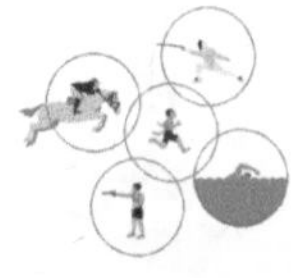

Pentathlon
Pentathlon

Marathon
Marathon

Saut à la perche
Pole vault

En plein air

Outdoor sports

Saut en hauteur
High jump

Saut en longueur
Long jump

Triple saut
Triple jump

Lancer du disque
Discus throw

Lancer du javelot
Javelin throw

Lancer du marteau
Hammer throw

Lancer du poids
Shot put

Ski alpin
Downhill skiing

Ski de fond
Cross-country skiing

Ski nordique
Nordic skiing

Snowboard
Snowboarding

Bobsleigh
Bobsleighing, bobsledding (US)

En plein air

Outdoor sports

Entraînement
Practice

Jeu
Game, match

Joueur
Player

Gagnant
Winner

Perdant
Loser

Victoire
Victory

Défaite
Defeat

Match nul, égalité
Draw, tie

Équipe
Team

Entraîneur
Trainer, coach

Arbitre
Referee

Règle
Rule

En plein air

Outdoor sports

Spectateur
Spectator

Supporter
Supporter

Stade
Stadium

Championnat
Championship

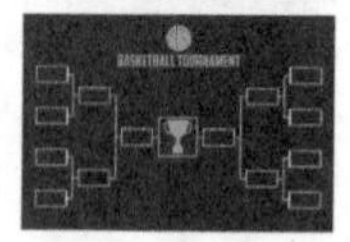

Tournoi
Tournament

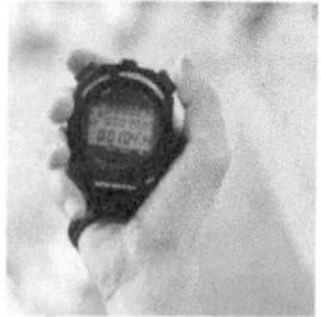

Chronomètre
Stopwatch

Démarrer
To start

S'entraîner
To practice

Marquer un point
To score a point

Gagner
To win

Perdre
To lose

Battre
To beat

En plein air

Outdoor sports

Phrases clés	Key phrases
Joues-tu au tennis ?	Do you play tennis?
J'aime courir tôt le matin.	I like to run early in the morning.
Je m'entraîne pour courir un marathon.	I'm training to run a marathon.
Je joue au volley-ball depuis cinq ans.	I have played volleyball for five years.
Au football, quand un joueur ne respecte pas les règles du jeu, l'arbitre peut donner un carton jaune ou un carton rouge.	In football (soccer), when a player doesn't follow the rules, the referee can give a yellow card or a red card.

En salle

Indoor sports

Judo
Judo

Karaté
Karate

Aïkido
Aikido

Kung fu
Kung fu

Gymnastique
Gymnastics

Escrime
Fencing

Bowling
Bowling

Boxe
Boxing

Lutte
Wrestling

Hockey
Field hockey

Hockey sur glace
Ice hockey

Racket-ball
Racquetball

En salle

Indoor sports

Haltérophilie
Weight-lifting

Danse
Dance

Phrases clés	Key phrases
J'aimerais savoir faire de la boxe, mais je n'ai jamais pris de cours.	I would love to know how to box, but I never took any lessons.
Vous devriez aller à un match de hockey sur glace quand vous serez au France.	You should go to an ice hockey game when you are in France.
Les jeux de boules est un sport très populaire en France.	Boules is a very popular sport in France.

Dans l'eau

Water sports

Natation
Swimming

Water-polo
Water polo

Aviron
Rowing

Voile
Sailing

Bateau à voile
Sail boat

Planche à voile
Windsurf, sailboard

Surf
Surfing

Planche de surf
Surfboard

Plongée avec tuba
Snorkeling

Plongée sous-marine
Scuba diving

Ski nautique
Water skiing

Kayak
Kayaking

Dans l'eau

Water sports

Rafting

Rafting

Phrases clés	Key phrases
Si vous visitez Paris ou Bordeaux, vous verrez peut-être l'équipe d'aviron s'entraîner.	If you're visiting Paris or Bordeaux, you might see the rowing team train.
Nous partons en Bretagne pour apprendre à surfer.	We're traveling to Brittany to learn to surf.
Y a-t-il un endroit pour faire du rafting dans les alentours ?	Is there a place to go rafting around here?
Je ne le savais pas, mais faire de la voile sur la Seine offre la meilleure vue de Paris.	I didn't know it, but sailing on the Seine gives the best view of Paris.

Le cinéma

The cinema

Cinéma
Cinema, movie theater

Film
Film, movie (US)

Court-métrage
Short film

Séance
Showing

Billet
Ticket

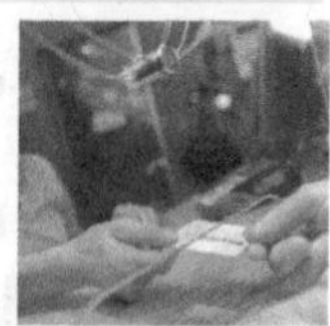

Guichet de cinéma
Box office

Kiosque à friandises
Concession stand

Écran
Screen

Fauteuil
Seat

Bande annonce
Trailer

Genre
Genre

Film d'action
Action movie

Le cinéma

The cinema

Comédie
Comedy

Drame
Drama

Film de science-fiction
Sci-fi movie

Film d'animation
Animated film

Film familial
Family movie

Monter
To edit

Film à grand succès
Blockbuster

Acteur
Actor

Actrice
Actress

Cascadeur, cascadeuse
Stunt actor/actress

Réalisateur, réalisatrice
Film director

Producteur, productrice
Film producer

Le cinéma

The cinema

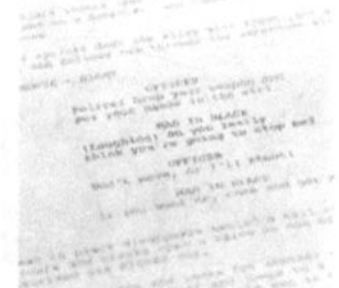

Scénario
Script

Public
Audience

Intrigue
Plot

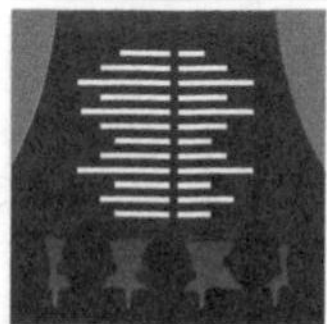

Générique
Credits

Doublage
Dubbing

Sous-titres
Subtitles

Aller au cinéma
To go to the cinema, to the movies (US)

Produire
To produce

Le cinéma

The cinema

Tourner
To shoot

Jouer
To play

Phrases clés	Key phrases
Quels films sont projetés aujourd'hui au cinéma ?	What movies are playing at the cinema today?
À quelle heure commence le film ?	What time does the film start?
Je n'aime pas les films d'action d'habitude, mais celui-ci était génial !	I don't usually like action movies, but this one was great!
J'adorerais aller au cinéma, mais je ne suis pas sûr(e) de comprendre s'il n'y a pas de sous-titres.	I'd love to go to the cinema, but I'm not sure I'll understand if there are no subtitles.
L'actrice principale jouait très bien !	The main actress played very well!
Le film est interdit aux moins de 17 ans, j'espère qu'il n'est pas trop violent.	The movie is rated R; I hope it's not too violent.

Le théâtre

The theatre

Théâtre
Theatre, theater (US)

Pièce de théâtre
Play

Billet
Ticket

Salle de théâtre
Playhouse

Loge
Box

Fauteuil
Seat

Orchestre, parterre
Pit

Balcon
Gallery

Poulailler/paradis
Gods (UK), peanut gallery (US)

Rideau
Curtain

Troupe
Company

Représentation
Performance

Le théâtre

The theatre

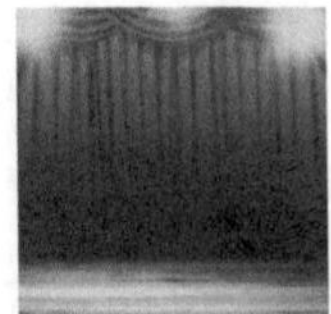

Scène
Stage

Acte
Act

Coulisses
Wings

Loge des artistes
Artists' dressing room

Décor
Scenery, set

Répétition
Rehearsal

Répétition générale
Dress rehearsal

Entracte
Interval, intermission

Comédien
Actor

Comédienne
Actress

Premier rôle
Leading part

Doublure
Understudy

Le théâtre

The theatre

Régisseur
Stage-manager

Accessoires
Props

Maquillage
Make-up

Costumier, costumière
Wardrobe-keeper

Trac
Stage fright

Jeux de scène
Stage business

Réplique
Line

Rappel
Curtain call

Jouer une pièce
To perform a play

Jouer un rôle
To play a part

Répéter
To rehearse

Mettre en scène
To direct, to stage

Le théâtre

The theatre

Distribuer les rôles
To cast a play

Entrer en scène
To come on the stage

Donner la réplique
To give the cue

Manquer la réplique
To miss the cue

Phrases clés	Key phrases
Cela fait des années que nous voulons voir cette pièce de théâtre.	We've been wanting to see this play for years!
L'acteur principal est malade donc sa doublure joue son rôle dans la représentation de ce soir.	The main actor is sick, so his understudy is playing his part in tonight's performance.
Nos fauteuils sont dans l'orchestre.	Our seats are in the pit (UK), orchestra seating (US).

L'opéra

The opera

Opéra
Opera

Opérette
Operetta

Avant-scène
Forestage

Arrière-scène
Back of the stage

Baignoire
Ground-floor box

Balcon
Balcony

Côté cour
Stage left

Côté jardin
Stage right

Éclairage
Lighting

Projecteur
Spotlight

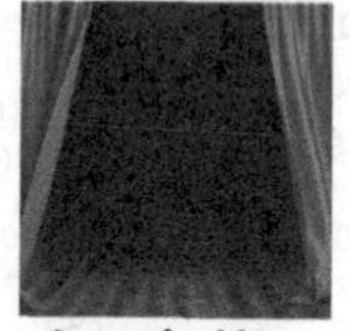

Lever de rideau
Raising of the curtain

Ouvreur, ouvreuse
Usher, usherette

L'opéra

The opera

Personnages
Characters

Aria
Aria

Baguette
Baton

Cadence
Cadenza

Coloratura
Coloratura

Livret
Libretto

Ouverture
Overture

Partition
Score

Surtitres
Supertitles

Baryton
Baritone

Basse
Bass

L'opéra

The opera

Contralto
Contralto

Mezzo-soprano
Mezzo-soprano

Soprano
Soprano

Ténor
Tenor

Chœur
Chorus

Chef de chœur
Chorus master

Compositeur
Composer

Chef d'orchestre
Conductor

Siffler
To whistle

Huer
To boo

L'opéra

The opera

Phrases clés	Key phrases
L'opéra que nous allons voir ce soir est très célèbre.	The opera we're seeing tonight is very famous.
Les chanteurs principaux sont une basse et une mezzo-soprano.	The main singers are a bass and a mezzo-soprano.
L'opéra a des surtitres car il est en italien.	The opera has supertitles because it is in Italian.

Le musée

The museum

Musée
Museum

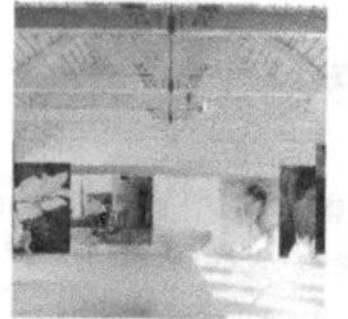

Galerie d'art
Gallery

Collection
Collection

Exposition
Exhibition

Tarif d'entrée
Admission fee

Tarif, prix
Fare

Don
Donation

Visite
Visit, tour

Vestiaire
Cloakroom

Art
Art

Conservateur
Curator

Guide touristique
Tour guide

Le musée
The museum

Visite guidée
Guided tour

Conservation
Preservation

Catalogue
Catalogue

Peinture, tableau
Painting

Peintre
Painter

Chef d'œuvre
Masterpiece

Cadre
Frame

Sculpture
Sculpture

Sculpteur
Sculptor

Céramique
Ceramic

Céramiste
Ceramist

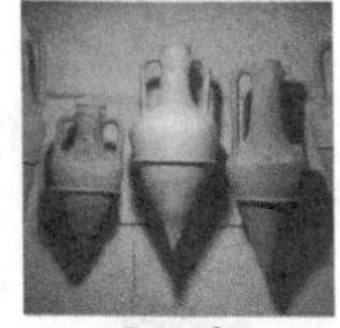

Poterie
Pottery

Le musée

The museum

Tapisserie
Tapestry

Aquarelle
Watercolor, aquarelle

Peinture à l'huile
Oil painting

Objet, artefact
Artefact (UK), artifact (US)

Boutique de souvenirs
Gift shop

Visiter
To visit

Réaliser, exécuter
To produce

Encadrer
To frame

Estimer
To appraise, to value, to assess

Exposer
To display, to show, to exhibit

Le musée

The museum

Phrases clés	Key phrases
Je veux visiter le Musée d'Orsay aujourd'hui.	I want to visit the Musée d'Orsay today.
Avez-vous été à l'exposition Picasso ?	Have you seen the Picasso exhibition?
Y a-t-il un droit d'entrée ?	Is there an admission charge?
À quelle heure fermez-vous ?	What time do you close?
Où puis-je avoir un audioguide ?	Where can I get an audioguide?
Excusez-moi, où se trouve le Mona Lisa ?	Excuse me, where is the Mona Lisa?
Est-il permis de prendre des photos dans le musée ?	Is it allowed to take pictures in the museum?

La musique

Music

Musique
Music

Note
Note

Touche
Key

Accord
Chord

Compositeur
Composer

Symphonie
Symphony

Orchestre
Orchestra

Chef d'orchestre
Conductor

Concert
Concert

Piano
Piano

Violon
Violin, fiddle

Archet
Bow

La musique

Music

Clavier
Keyboard

Clavecin
Harpsichord

Instruments à cordes
String instruments

Alto
Viola

Cello
Violoncelle

Contrebasse
Double-bass

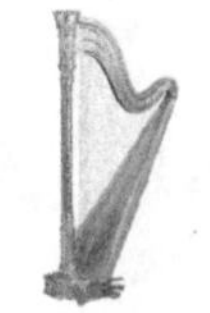

Harpe
Harp

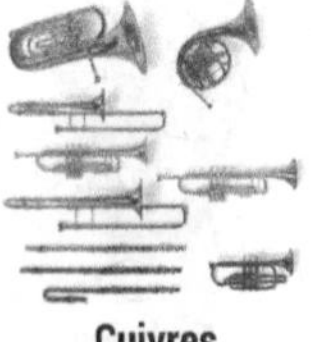

Cuivres
Brass

Instruments à vent
Wind instruments

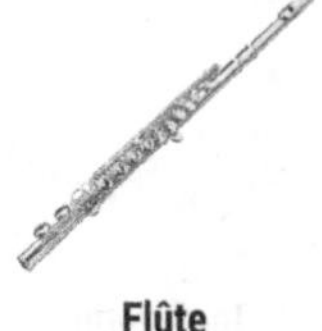

Flûte
Flute

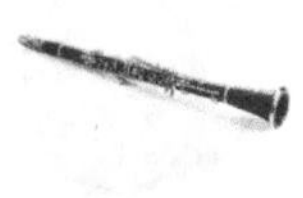

Clarinette
Clarinet

Hautbois
Oboe

La musique
Music

Trompette
Trumpet

Trombone
Trombone

Cor
Horn

Saxophone
Saxophone, sax

Tuba
Tuba

Instruments à percussion
Percussion instruments

Tambour
Drum

Timbales
Kettle-drums, timpani, drums

Cymbales
Cymbals

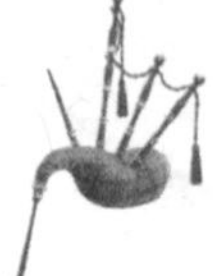

Cornemuse
Bagpipe

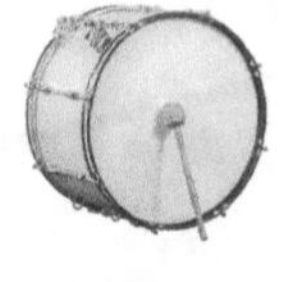

Grosse caisse
Big drum

Tambourin
Tambourine

La musique

Music

Harmonica
Harmonica

Batterie
Drum kit

Guitare acoustique
Acoustic guitar

Guitare électrique
Electric guitar

Orgue
Organ

Chant
Singing

Chanson
Song

Chœur
Choir

Paroles
Lyrics

Air
Tune

Couplet
Verse

Refrain
Chorus

La musique

Music

Jouer d'un instrument
To play an instrument

S'exercer
To practise (UK), to practice (US)

Faire des gammes
To play scales

Racler
To scrape

Jouer juste
To play in tune

Jouer faux
To play out of tune

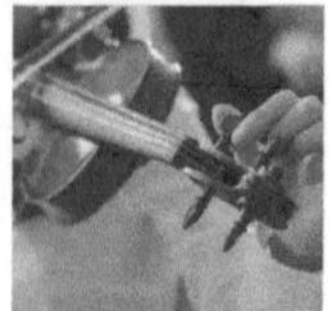

Accorder
To tune

Frapper, toucher
To strike

Pincer (les cordes)
To pluck

Exécuter un morceau
To perform a piece

Suivre la cadence, être en mesure
To keep time

La musique

Music

Phrases clés	Key phrases
Est-ce que tu sais jouer de la guitare ?	Do you know how to play the guitar?
Je peux jouer du piano, du violon et du violoncelle.	I can play the piano, the violin and the cello.
Elle peut chanter à la perfection mais elle ne joue d'aucun instrument.	She can sing perfectly, but she doesn't play an instrument.
Il s'exerce pendant deux heures chaque jour.	He practices two hours every day.

En cas d'urgence

In case of emergencies

La description du corps

Body parts

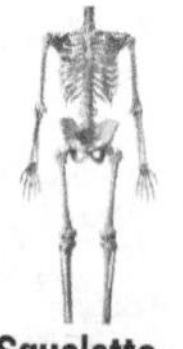

Squelette
Skeleton

Os
Bone

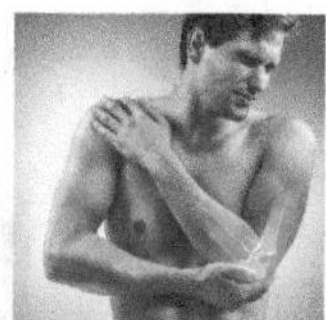

Articulation
Joint

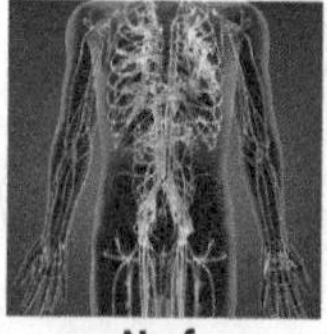

Nerf
Nerve

Muscle
Muscle

Chair
Flesh

Peau
Skin

Tête
Head

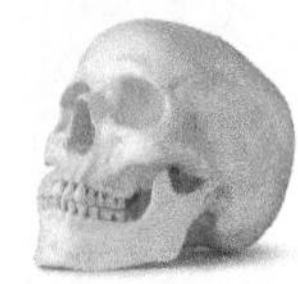

Crâne
Skull

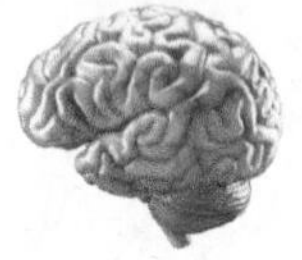

Cerveau
Brain

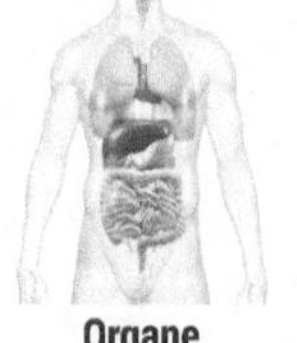

Organe
Organ

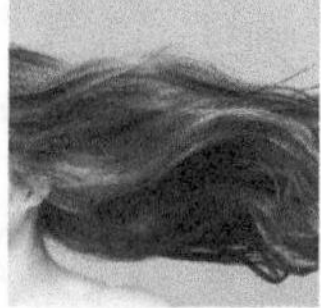

Cheveux
Hair

La description du corps

Body parts

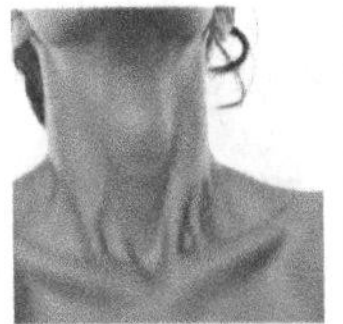

Cou
Neck

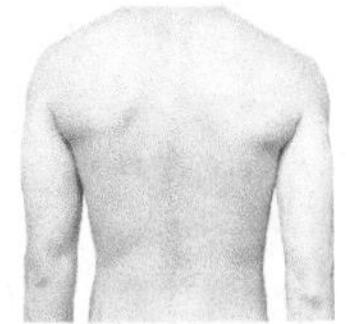

Dos
Back

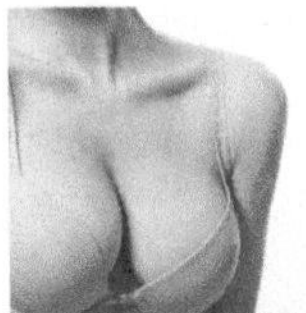

Poitrine, sein
Breast

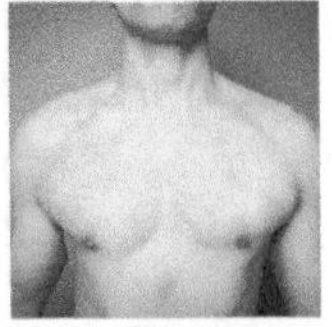

Cage thoracique
Chest

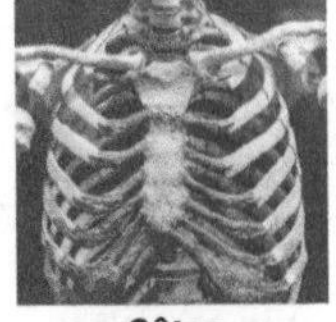

Côtes
Ribs

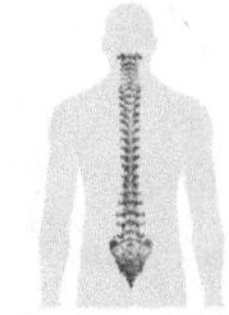

Colonne vertébrale
Backbone, spine

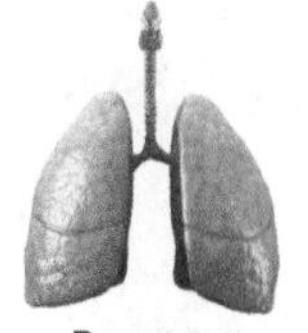

Poumons
Lungs

Cœur
Heart

Sang
Blood

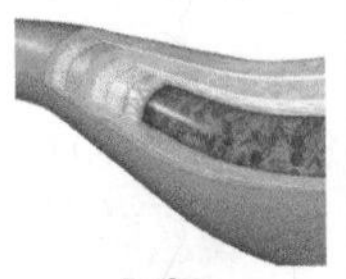

Artère
Artery

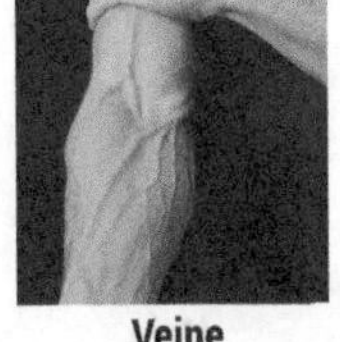

Veine
Vein

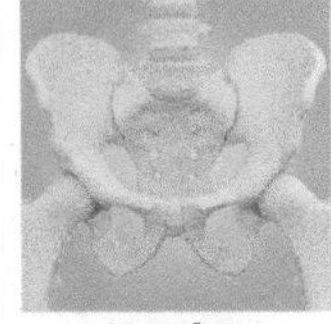

Hanches
Hips

La description du corps

Body parts

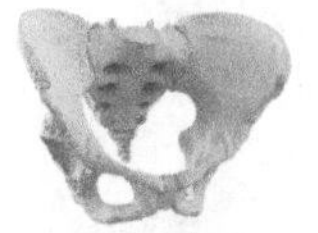

Bassin
Pelvis

Foie
Liver

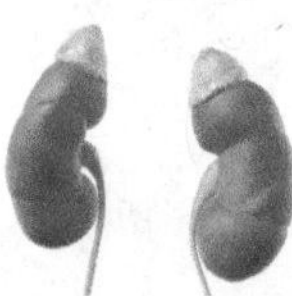

Rein
Kidney

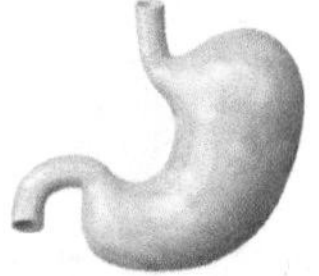

Estomac
Stomach

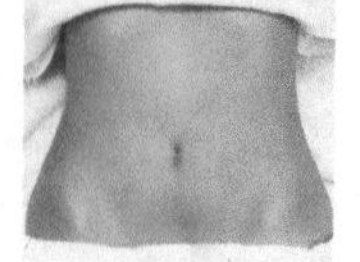

Ventre, abdomen
Belly

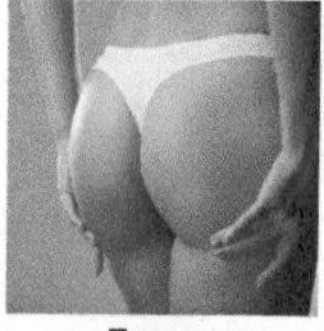

Fesses
Buttocks, bottom, backside

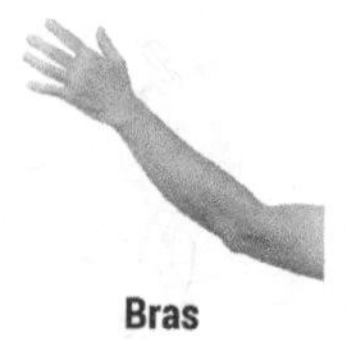

Bras
Arm

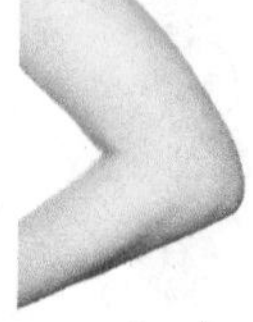

Coude
Elbow

Poignet
Wrist

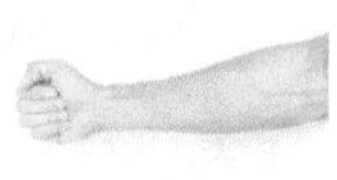

Avant-bras
Forearm

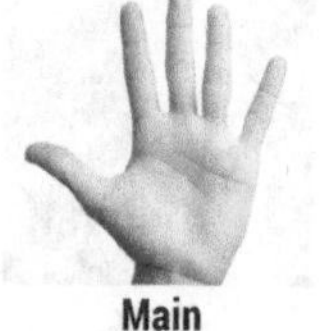

Main
Hand

Doigt
Finger

La description du corps

Body parts

Pouce
Thumb

Poing
Fist

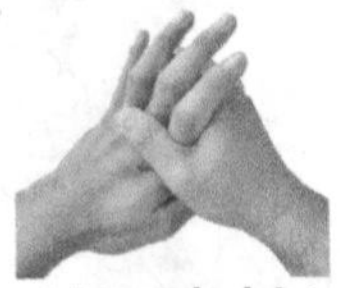

Jointure du doigt
Knuckles

Jambe
Leg

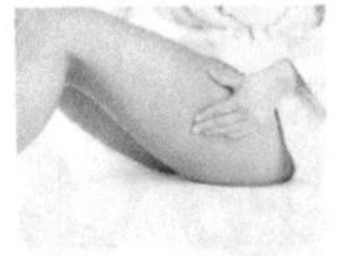

Cuisse
Thigh

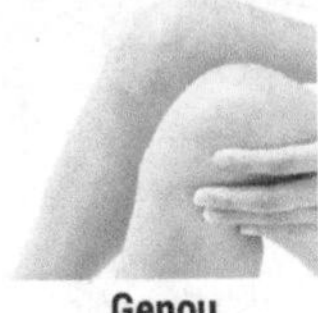

Genou
Knee

Tibia
Shin

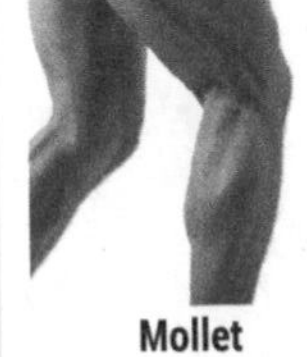

Mollet
Calf

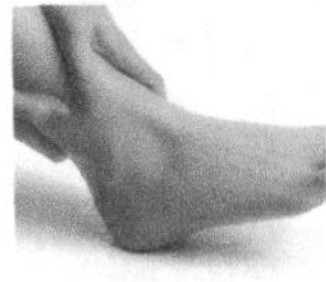

Cheville
Ankle

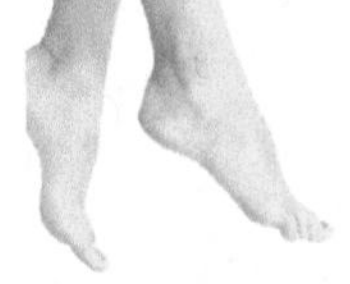

Pied (pieds)
Foot (feet)

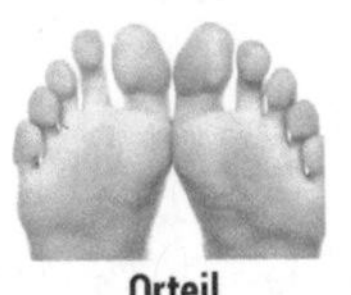

Orteil
Toe

Plante du pied
Sole

La description du corps

Body parts

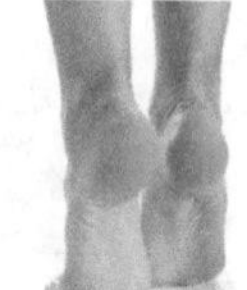

Talon
Heel

Respirer
To breathe

(S') Étouffer
To suffocate

(S') Étrangler
To choke

Battre
To beat

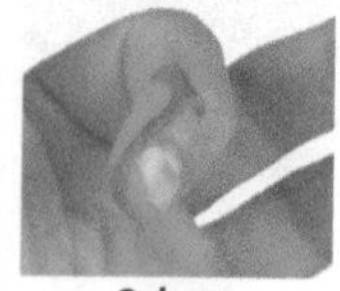

Saigner
To bleed

La description du visage

Face parts

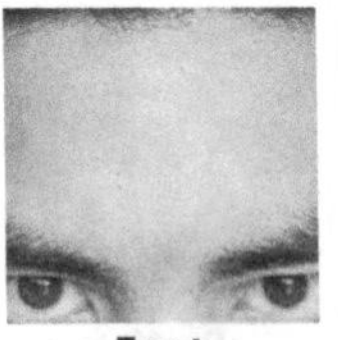

Front
Forehead, brow

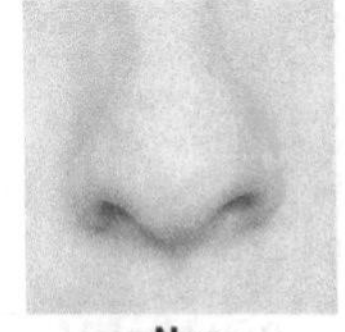

Nez
Nose

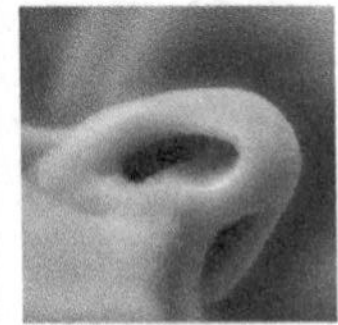

Narine
Nostril

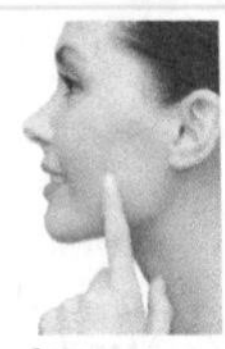

Joue
Cheek

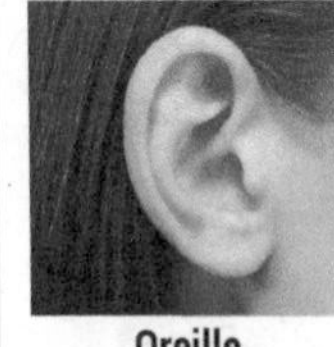

Oreille
Ear

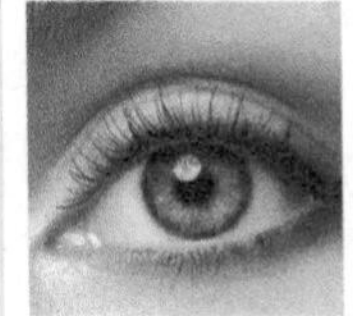

Œil
Eye

Sourcil
Eyebrow

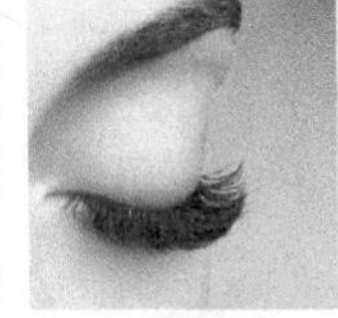

Cils
Eyelashes

Paupière
Eyelid

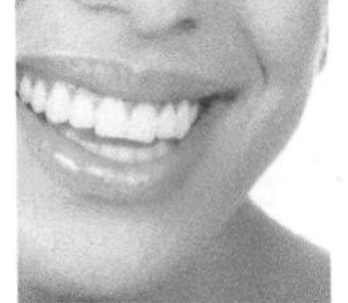

Bouche
Mouth

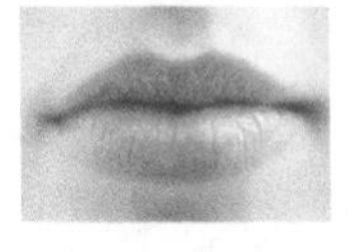

Lèvre
Lip

Lèvre supérieure
Upper lip

La description du visage

Face parts

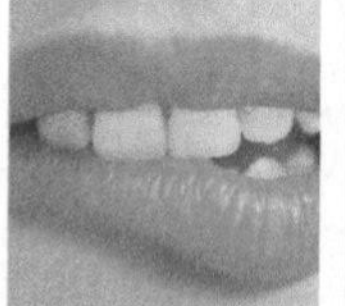

Lèvre inférieure
Lower lip

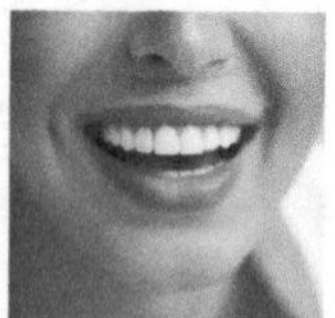

Dent (dents)
Tooth (teeth)

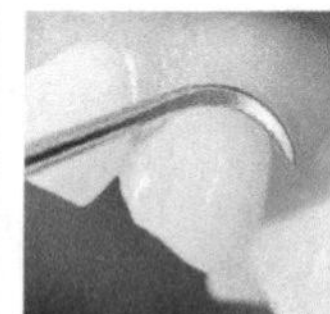

Gencive
Gum

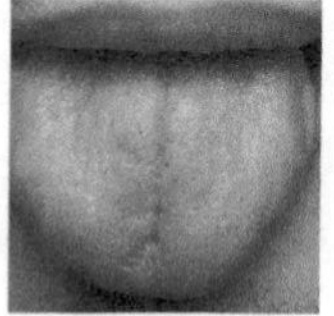

Langue
Tongue

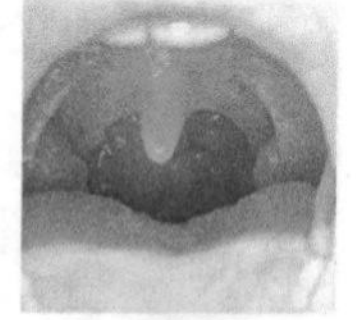

Palais
Palate

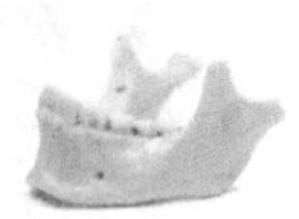

Mâchoire
Jaw

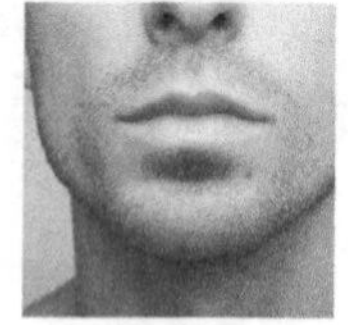

Menton
Chin

Pommette
Cheekbone

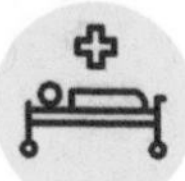

Le médecin

The doctor

Médecin généraliste
General practitioner, GP

Patient, malade
Patient

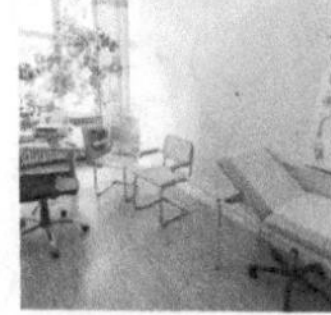

Cabinet médical
Surgery (UK), doctor's office (US)

Salle d'attente
Waiting room

Assurance maladie
Health insurance

Maladie
Disease

Douleur
Pain

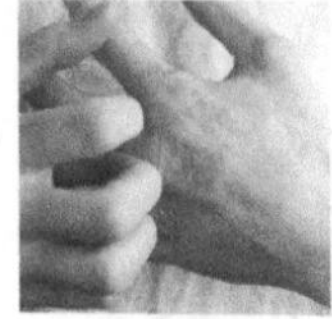

État
Condition

Ordonnance
Prescription

Traitement
Treatment

Effets secondaires
Side effects

Symptômes
Symptoms

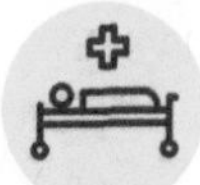

Le médecin

The doctor

Fièvre
Fever

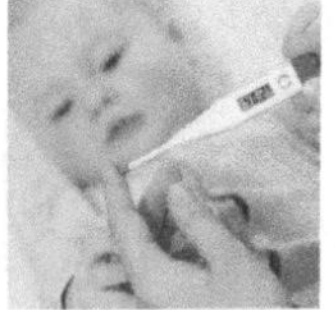

Température
Temperature

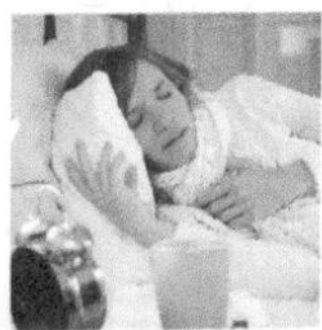

Grippe
Flu

Rhume
Cold

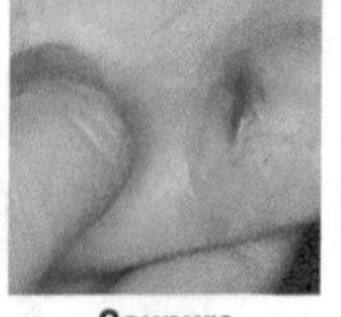

Coupure
Cut

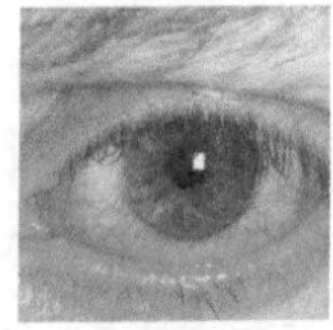

Conjonctivite
Eye infection

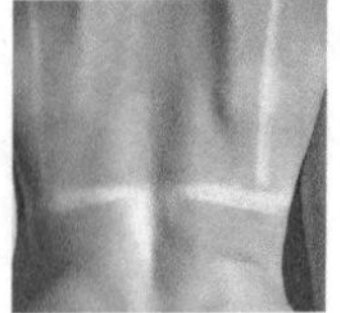

Coup de soleil
Sunburn

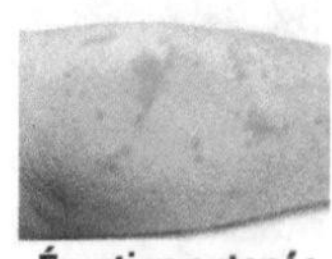

Éruption cutanée
Skin rash

Consulter un médecin
To consult a doctor

Prendre la température
To take one's temperature

Être malade
To be sick, to be ill

Faire mal
To hurt

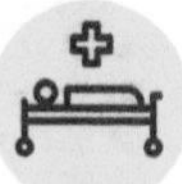

Le médecin

The doctor

Attraper un rhume
To catch a cold

Tousser
To cough

Éternuer
To sneeze

Vomir
To vomit

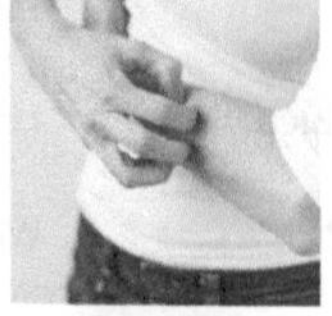

Se gratter
To scratch

S'évanouir
To faint

Avoir mal à la gorge
To have a sore throat

Avoir mal au dos
To have a backache

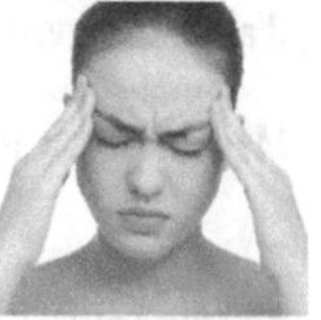

Avoir mal à la tête
To have a headache

Avoir mal aux dents
To have a toothache

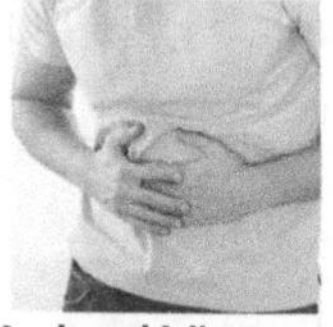

Avoir mal à l'estomac
To have a stomachache

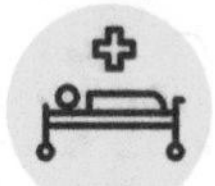

Le médecin

The doctor

Phrases clés	Key phrases
Je voudrais prendre rendez-vous, s'il vous plaît.	I would like to make an appointment, please.
Puis-je venir ce matin ?	Can I come this morning?
Je ne me sens pas bien.	I don't feel well.
Où avez-vous mal ?	Where does it hurt?
Mon dos me fait mal.	My back hurts.
J'ai de la fièvre.	I have a fever.
Mes allergies se réveillent !	My allergies are acting up!
Je vais vérifier votre tension.	I'm going to check your blood pressure.
Je vais vous faire une ordonnance.	I'll write you a prescription.

Pharmacie et médicaments

The pharmacy and medicines

Pharmacy
Pharmacy, drugstore

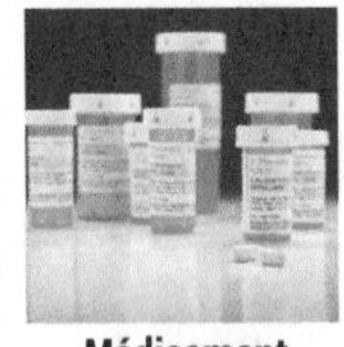

Médicament
Medicine, drug

Pharmacienne
Chemist, pharmacist (US)

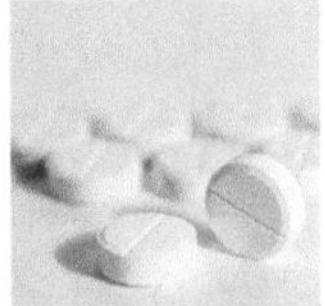

Comprimé
Tablet

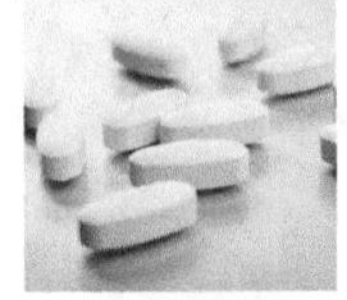

Pilule
Pill

Gélule
Capsule

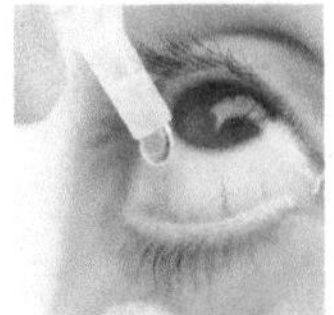

Goutte
Drop

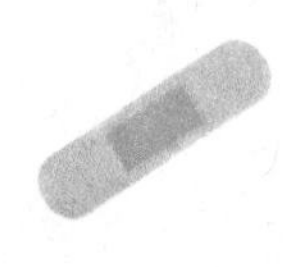

Pansement adhésif
Band-Aid

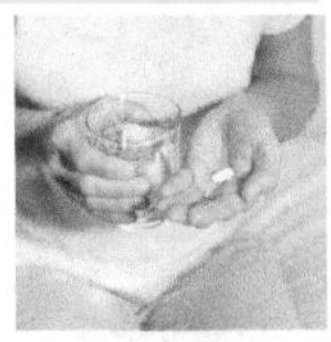

Antalgique
Painkiller

Aspirine
Aspirin

Calmant
Tranquilizer

Pastilles pour la toux
Cough drops

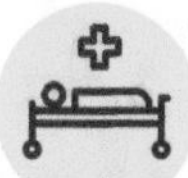

Pharmacie et médicaments

The pharmacy and medicines

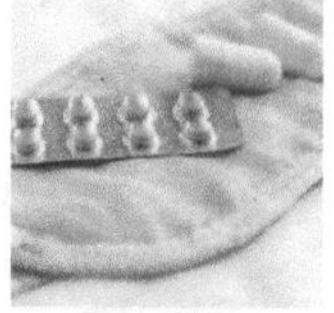

Somnifère
Sleeping pill

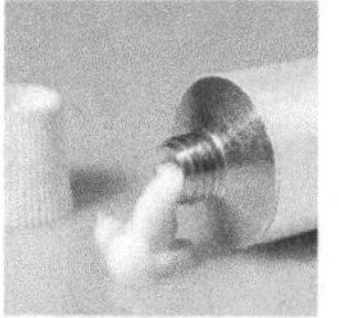

Pommade
Ointment

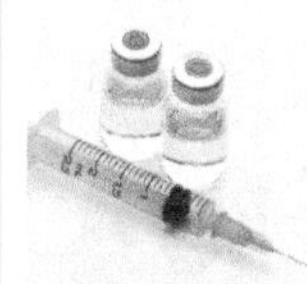

Piqûre
Injection

Bandage
Bandage

Vitamines
Vitamins

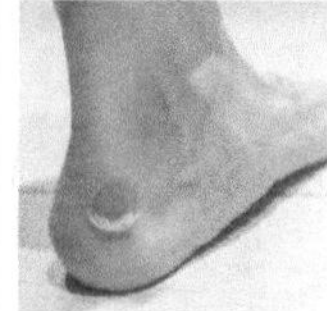

Ampoule
Blister

Prendre des médicaments
To take drugs/medications

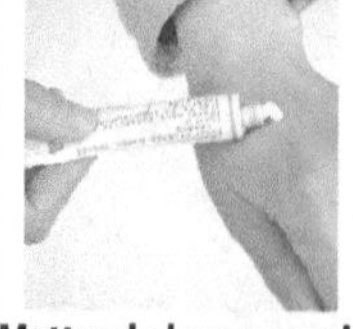

Mettre de la pommade
To put on ointment

Prendre du repos
To get some rest

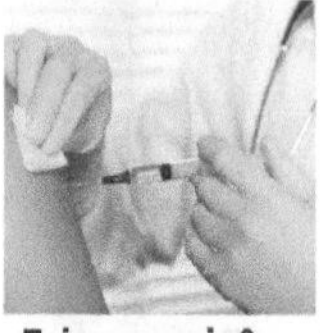

Faire une piqûre
To give an injection

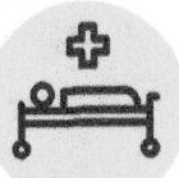

L'hôpital

The hospital

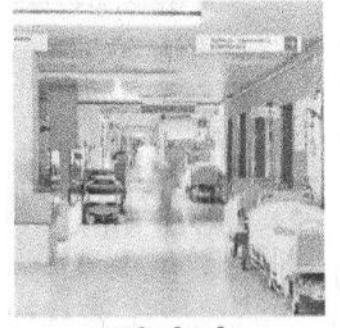

Hôpital
Hospital

Clinique
Clinic

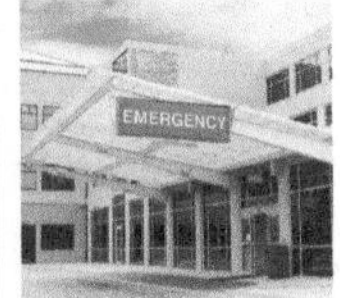

Urgence
Emergency room

Chirurgien.ne
Surgeon

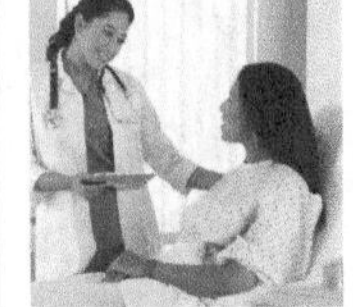

Médecin
Physician

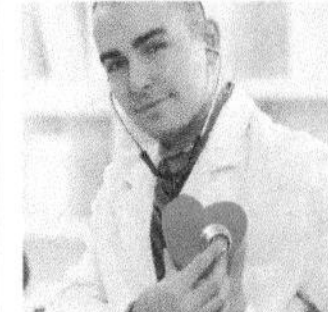

Cardiologue
Cardiologist

Anesthésiste
Anaesthetist, anesthesiologist (US)

Dentiste
Dentist

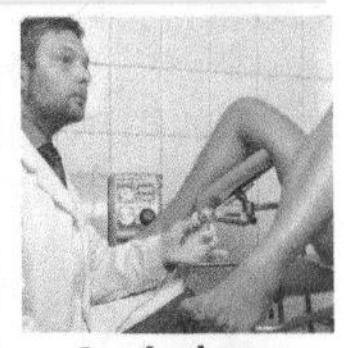

Gynécologue
Gynaecologist, gynocologist (US)

Pneumologue
Lung specialist

Oto-rhyno-laryngologiste (ORL)
Nose and throat specialist

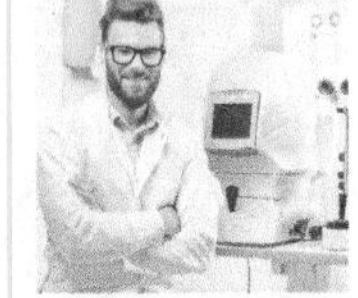

Ophtalmologue
Ophthalmologist

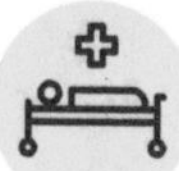

L'hôpital

The hospital

Sage-femme, maïeuticien
Midwife

Infirmier, infimière
Nurse

Accident
Accident

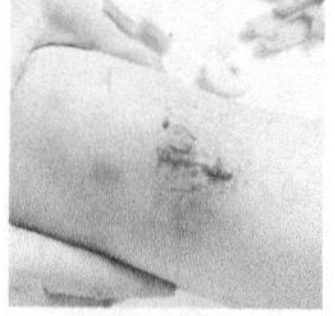

Blessure
Wound, injury

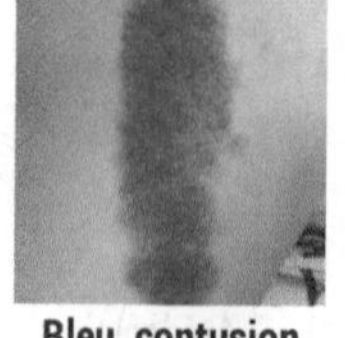

Bleu, contusion
Bruise

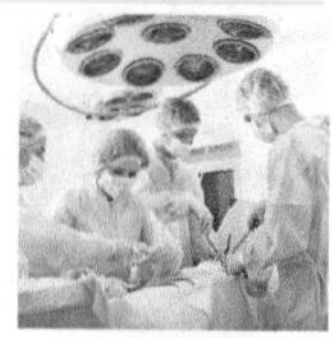

Chirurgie
Surgery

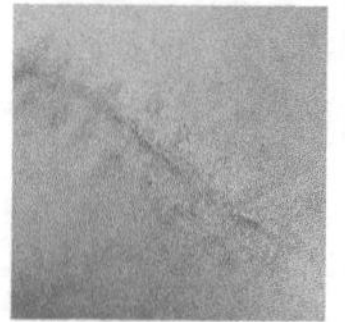

Cicatrice
Scar

Crise cardiaque
Heart attack

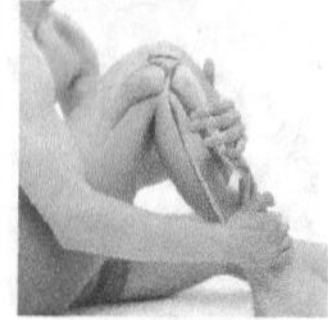

Os fracturé
Broken bone

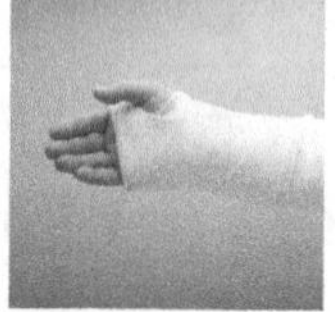

Plâtre
Plaster

Brûlure
Burn

Diarrhée
Diarrhea

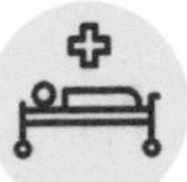

L'hôpital
The hospital

Intoxication alimentaire
Food poisoning

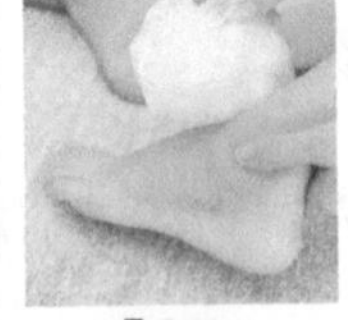

Entorse
Sprain

Échantillon d'urine
Urine sample

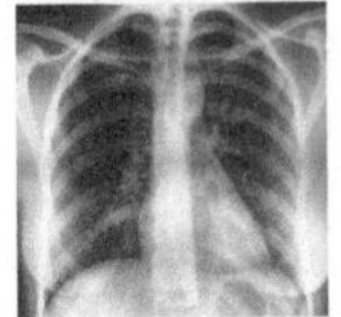

Radiographie
X-ray

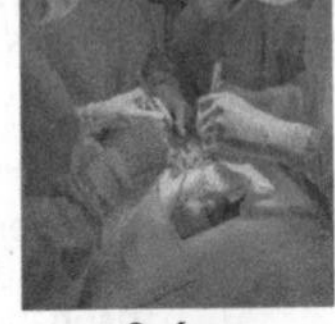

Opérer
To operate on

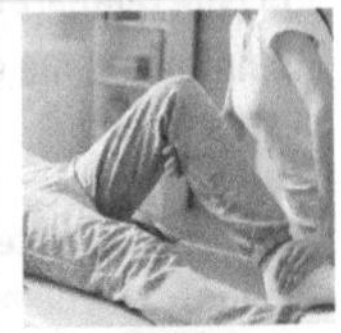

Soigner
To heal

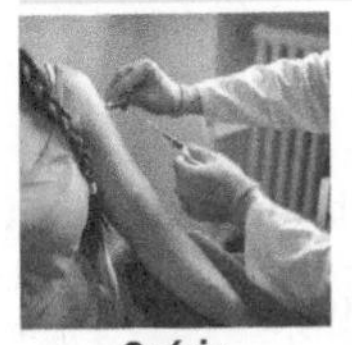

Guérir
To cure

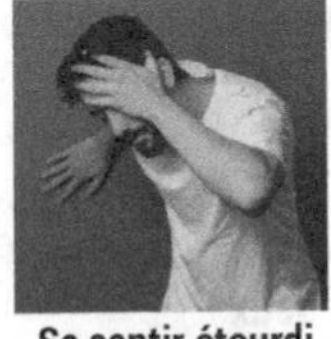

Se sentir étourdi
To feel dizzy

Se sentir nauséeux
To feel nauseous

Être contagieux
To be contagious

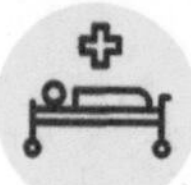

L'hôpital

The hospital

Phrases clés	Key phrases
Aidez-moi, je me suis fait mordre par un serpent !	Help me, I was bitten by a snake!
Je suis tombé(e) et maintenant, ma cheville est enflée.	I fell down, and now my ankle is swollen.
Ça fait une heure que je vomis, je ne comprends pas ce qui se passe.	I've been vomiting for an hour; I don't know what's happening.
Votre état n'est pas inquiétant.	Your condition is not worrying.
Vos symptômes devraient disparaître complètement d'ici deux jours.	Your symptoms should disappear completely within two days.
Il va falloir vous opérer.	You're going to need surgery.

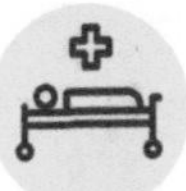

La police

The police

Police
Police

Poste de police
Police station

Agent de police
Policeman, constable, cop

Renseignements
Information

Voiture de police
Patrol car

Menottes
Handcuffs

Matraque
Baton

Casquette de police
Police hat

Insigne de police
Police badge

Commissaire de police
Police captain

Lieutenant de police
Police lieutenant

Pistolet
Handgun

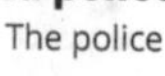

La police
The police

Sifflet
Whistle

Gilet pare-balles
Bulletproof vest

Enquête
Investigation

Meutre
Murder

Trafic de drogue
Drug trafficking

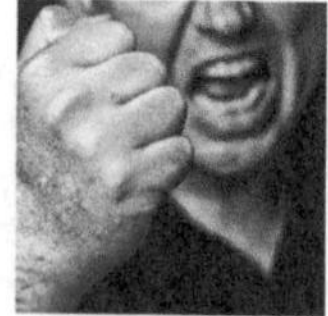

Menace
Threat

Accident
Accident

Attaque
Attack

Agression
Assault

Vol
Theft

Perte
Loss

Disparition
Disappearance

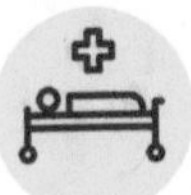

La police

The police

Suspect
Suspect

P.V., amende
Ticket

Indice
Clue

Preuve
Evidence

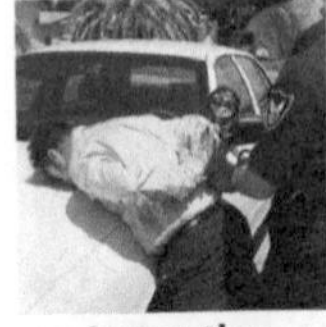

Arrestation
Arrest

Fouille
Search

Mandat de perquisition
Search warrant

Interrogatoire
Interrogation

Aveux
Confession

Garde à vue
Custody

Appeler la police
To call the police

Être de service
To be on duty

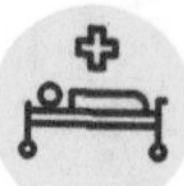

La police
The police

Ne pas être de service
To be off duty

Demander son chemin
To ask one's way

Signaler
To report

Enquêter
To investigate

Mener une enquête
To conduct an investigation

Soupçonner
To suspect

Arrêter
To arrest

Interroger
To question

Avouer
To confess

Relâcher
To release

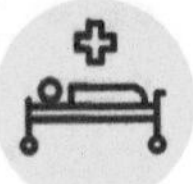

La police
The police

Phrases clés	Key phrases
Comment puis-je contacter la police ?	How can I contact the police?
Mon portefeuille a été volé, que dois-je faire ?	My wallet has been stolen; what do I do?
On est entré par effraction dans la maison.	The house has been broken into.
J'ai été témoin d'une agression.	I witnessed an assault.
Nous sommes en train d'interroger quelques suspects.	We're questioning some suspects.
Quelqu'un a avoué pendant la garde à vue.	Someone confessed while in custody.

Les pompiers/l'ambulance

The firefighters/the ambulance

Pompiers
Fire brigade

Pompe à incendie
Fire engine

Échelle
Ladder

Tuyau
Hose

Bouche d'incendie
Hydrant, fire-plug

Extincteur
Fire extinguisher

Sortie de secours
Emergency exit

Exercice d'alerte au feu
Fire drill

Ambulance
Ambulance

Ambulancier, ambulancière
Ambulance driver, ambulance man/woman

Civière
Stretcher

Mettre le feu à quelque chose
To set something on fire

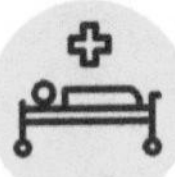

Les pompiers/l'ambulance

The firefighters/the ambulance

Brûler, incendier
To burn down

Éteindre un incendie
To put out a fire

Sauver une victime
To rescue a victim

Se sauver
To escape

Phrases clés	Key phrases
Au feu !	Fire!
Appelez une ambulance !	Call an ambulance!
Il y a encore des gens à l'intérieur du bâtiment !	There still are people inside the building!

Chapter 01

Page 16: alice_photo/Adobe Stock Photos, Racle Fotodesign/Adobe Stock Photos, Monkey Business/Adobe Stock Photos, pressmaster/Adobe Stock Photos, RioPatuca Images/Adobe Stock Photos, dell/Adobe Stock Photos, jlaatz/Pixabay, Nel_Botha-NZ/Pixabay, adisa/Adobe Stock Photos, BillionPhotos.com/Adobe Stock Photos, monticellllo/Adobe Stock Photos, pxhere.

Page 17: sumroeng/Adobe Stock Photos, Wikimedia, Inkara/Adobe Stock Photos, Artem/Adobe Stock Photos, Francesco Scatena/Adobe Stock Photos, Rawpixel.com/Adobe Stock Photos, Rawpixel.com/Adobe Stock Photos.

Page 19: ismail mohamed - SoviLe/Unsplash, gstockstudio/Adobe Stock Photos, Pixabay, euthymia/Adobe Stock Photos, nadezhda1906/Adobe Stock Photos, vitaliymateha/Adobe Stock Photos, Maksym Dragunov/Adobe Stock Photos, Lotfi MATTOU/Adobe Stock Photos, italita/Adobe Stock Photos, Falcon Eyes/Adobe Stock Photos, Pixabay, Carlos Yudica/Adobe Stock Photo.

Page 20: iStockphoto/Getty Images, Josh/Pexels, wemm/Adobe Stock Photos, Stephen Davies/Adobe Stock Photos.

Page 22: kameraauge/Adobe Stock Photos, Scanrail/Adobe Stock Photos, Iurii Davydov/Shutterstock, mayabuns/Adobe Stock Photos, Scanrail/Adobe Stock Photos, Nikolai Sorokin/Adobe Stock Photos, Elizaveta/Adobe Stock Photos, Paylessimages/Adobe Stock Photos, Marcus Wong Wongm/Wikimedia, Garry Basnett/Adobe Stock Photos, jdoms/Adobe Stock Photos, CNF/Adobe Stock Photos.

Page 23: Shiny777/Adobe Stock Photos, Shiny777/Adobe Stock Photos, lucamato/Adobe Stock Photos, Khun Ta/Adobe Stock Photos, auremar/Adobe Stock Photos, Wikimedia, h368k742/Adobe Stock Photos, Shiny777/Adobe Stock Photos, WavebreakMediaMicro/Adobe Stock Images, Sven Grundmann/Adobe Stock Photos, Andrew Brown/Wikimedia.

Page 25: xbrchx/Adobe Stock Photos, Mathias P.R. Reding/Unsplash, ALEKSTOCK.COM/Adobe Stock Photos, James Steidl/Adobe Stock Photos, Peruphotoart/Adobe Stock Photos, Alex

Tihonovs/Shutterstock, Yakobchuk Olena/Adobe Stock Photos, chingyunsong/Adobe Stock Photos, Wikimedia Commons, Genesis12/Wikimedia Commons, doomu/Adobe Stock Photos, Thomas Bethge/Adobe Stock Photos.

Page 26: stp23/Adobe Stock Photos, Philip Kock/UnSplash, Vincent Bouchet/Adobe Stock Photos, nerthuz/Adobe Stock Photos, Brandon Klein/Adobe Stock Photos, gonin/Adobe Stock Photos, Andrii /Adobe Stock Photos, Syda Productions/ Adobe Stock Photos, Monkey Business/Adobe Stock Photos.

Page 28: Konstantinos Moraiti/Adobe Stock Photos, Oleg/Adobe Stock Photos, Jürgen Fälchle/Adobe Stock Photos, cristianstorto/ Adobe Stock Photos, Piman Khrutmuang/Adobe Stock Photos, rh2010/Adobe Stock Photos, Creativa Images/Shutterstock, Maksim Toome/Adobe Stock Photos, filmbildfabrik/Adobe Stock Photos, boophuket/Adobe Stock Photos, black_magic/Adobe Stock Photos, Destina/Adobe Stock Photos.

Page 29: supergenijalac/Shutterstock.com, serikbaib/Adobe Stock Photos, Angelov/Adobe Stock Photos, Wikimedia Commons, Alx/Adobe Stock Photos, GTeam/Adobe Stock Photos, birdlkportfolio2559/Adobe Stock Photos, Gudellaphoto/Adobe Stock Photos, Gudellaphoto/Adobe Stock Photos, Gudellaphoto/Adobe Stock Photos, Wikimedia Commons, Ayzek/Adobe Stock Photos.

Page 30: chuck1964/Adobe Stock Photos, accurate_shot/ Adobe Stock Photos, Wonderful pictures/Adobe Stock Photos, Ye Liew/Shutterstock, zirconicusso/Adobe Stock Photos, accurate_shot/Adobe Stock Photos, bedya/Adobe Stock Photos, Moose/Adobe Stock Photos, sema_srinouljan/Adobe Stock Photos, Wikimedia Commons, Rasulov/Adobe Stock Photos, krispetkong/Adobe Stock Photos.

Page 31: mipan/Adobe Stock Photos, Capri23auto/5807 images/ Pixabay, Wikimedia Commons, Lisa F. Young/Adobe Stock Photos, weerapat1003/Adobe Stock Photos, piyaphunjun/Adobe Stock Photos, Oleksii Nykonchuk/Adobe Stock Photos, daniiD/ Adobe Stock Photos, fazon/Adobe Stock Photos, Robert Bye/ UnSplash, Paylessimages/Adobe Stock Photos, neiezhmakov/ Adobe Stock Photos.

Page 32: Wikimedia Commons, Wikimedia Commons, Debbie Ann Powell/Adobe Stock Photos, moodboard/Adobe Stock Photos, Wikimedia Commons, ほじん/Adobe Stock Photos, inimma/Adobe Stock Photos, z1b/Adobe Stock Photos, sp4764/Adobe Stock Photos, Jonathan Billinger/Wikimedia commons, Hans M/UnSplash, SPUI/Wikimedia.

Page 33: Wikimedia Commons, benjaminnolte/Adobe Stock Photos, Ivan/Adobe Stock Photos, Lisa F. Young/Adobe Stock Photos, am/Adobe Stock Photos, Wikimedia Commons, New Africa/Adobe Stock Photos.

Page 35: tournee/Adobe Stock Photos, Kzenon/Adobe Stock Photos, tournee/Adobe Stock Photos, Simon Coste/Adobe Stock Photos, Tomasz Zajda/Adobe Stock Photos, milkovasa/Adobe Stock Photos, Mat Hayward/Adobe Stock Photos.

Page 37: stockphoto-graf/Adobe Stock Photos, stockphoto-graf/Adobe Stock Photos, rotoGraphics/Adobe Stock Photos, ia_64/Adobe Stock Photos, ugurmuldur/Adobe Stock Photos, nito/Adobe Stock Photos, stockphoto-graf/Adobe Stock Photos, amnarj2006/Adobe Stock Photos, MIH83/494 images/Pixabay, Ambartsumian/Adobe Stock Photos, moonrise/Adobe Stock Photos, lastfurianec/Adobe Stock Photos.

Page 38: OceanProd/Adobe Stock Photos, Winai Tepsuttinun/Adobe Stock Photos, Jiri Hera/Adobe Stock Photos, Georgy Dzyura/Adobe Stock Photos, Elizaveta/Adobe Stock Photos, Photobeps/Adobe Stock Photos, moonrise/Adobe Stock Photos, ipopba/Adobe Stock Photos, Dmytro Panchenko/Adobe Stock Photos, Richard Villalon/Adobe Stock Photos, nkarol/Adobe Stock Photos, PUNTOSTUDIOFOTO Lda/Adobe Stock Photos.

Page 39: zinkevych/Adobe Stock Photos, phototromeo/Adobe Stock Photos, KissShot/Adobe Stock Photos.

Chapter 02

Page 42: Cookie Studio/Adobe Stock Photos, be free/Adobe Stock Photos, Cookie Studio/Adobe Stock Photos, Grispb/Adobe Stock Photos, detailblick-foto/Adobe Stock Photos.

Page 45: michaelheim/Adobe Stock Photos, Victor Koldunov/ Adobe Stock Photos.

Page 46: Maridav/Adobe Stock Photos, william87/Adobe Stock Photos, shurkin_son/Adobe Stock Photos, Roman Babakin/ Adobe Stock Photos.

Page 47: pathdoc/Adobe Stock Photos, Viacheslav Iakobchuk/ Adobe Stock Photos.

Chapter 03

Page 50: Pexels, jLasWilson/225 images/Pixabay, Rawpixel.com/Adobe Stock Photo.

Page 51: jojoo64/Adobe Stock Photos, PictureP./Adobe Stock Photos, PictureP./Adobe Stock Photos, jojoo64/Adobe Stock Photos, jojoo64/Adobe Stock Photos, Pexels, Lotus Head/Wikimedia Commons, khosrork/Adobe Stock Photos, M.studio/ Adobe Stock Photos, MemoryCatcher/4691 images/Pixabay, Grafissimo/Getty Images, CLIPAREA.com/Adobe Stock Photos.

Page 52: Martino Pietropoli on Unsplash, vladimirfloyd/Adobe Stock Photos, jojoo64/Adobe Stock Photos, Dmytro/Adobe Stock Photos, mantinov/Adobe Stock Photos.

Page 54: Sergii Figurnyi/Adobe Stock Photos, Indolences/Wikimedia Commons, Faizat/Adobe Stock Photos, Peter Brewer/ Adobe Stock Photos, Kirk Fisher/Adobe Stock Photos, Wikimedia Commons, Daniel Lobo/Wikimedia Commons, Pexels, Donnerbold/Adobe Stock Photos, cantor pannatto/Adobe Stock Photos, ursule/Adobe Stock Photos, kuma/Adobe Stock Photos.

Page 55: Makalu / 2383 images/Pixabay, IDuke/Wikimedia Commons, Алексей Сергеев/Adobe Stock Photos, Sebastian Ballard/Wikimedia Commons, Free-Photos/9080 images/ Pixabay, Colin/Wikimedia Commons, Gilberto Mesquita/Adobe Stock Photos, Pixabay, Ferita/Adobe Stock Photos, J. Ligero Loarte/Wikimedia Commons.

Page 57: Wikimedia Commons, Pixabay, Wikimedia Commons, Paasikivi/Wikimedia Commons, Wikimedia Commons,

Wikimedia Commons, Beyond My Ken/Wikimedia Commons, UnSplash, Ruslan/Adobe Stock Photos, Pexels, 4th Life Photography/Adobe Stock Photos, Pexels.

Page 58: Diliff/Wikimedia Commons, Diliff/Wikimedia Commons, nievesmares/Adobe Stock Photos, EvaBergschneider/7 images/Pixabay, Dmitry Vereshchagin/Adobe Stock Photos, Wikimedia Commons, Flayas/Wikimedia Commons, demerzel21/Adobe Stock Photos, JK/Adobe Stock Photos, Bruno Bleu/Adobe Stock Photos, Guilhem Vellut/Wikimedia Commons, Sundry Photography/Adobe Stock Photos.

Page 59: Kev Maltese-Crottier/Adobe Stock Photos, JingSun/10 Bilder/Pixabay, Bjørn Christian Tørrissen/Wikimedia Commons, Pexels, mark penny/Adobe Stock Photos, Al Ianni/Wikimedia Commons, ShinyChunks/Adobe Stock Photos, Wikimedia Commons, Andrzej Barabasz/Wikimedia Commons, Benh LIEU SONG/Wikimedia Commons, salah/Adobe Stock Photos, dbrnjhrj/Adobe Stock Photos.

Page 60: Diliff/Wikimedia Commons, Rdevany/Wikimedia Commons, Alexander Johmann/Flicker, Wikimedia Commons, Dietmar Rabich/Wikimedia Commons, Benh LIEU SONG/Wikimedia Commons, pierre9x6/135 images/Pixabay, Wikimedia Commons.

Page 62: denboma/Adobe Stock Photos, Steven Miller/Flicker, Steven Miller/Flicker, Bits and Splits/Adobe Stock Photos, Jackin/Adobe Stock Photos, naiauss/Adobe Stock Photos, khuruzero/Adobe Stock Photos, zilber42/Adobe Stock Photos, Galdric Penarroja/ADDICTIVE STOCK/Adobe Stock Photos, phototouch/Adobe Stock Photos, martine wagner/Adobe Stock Photos, Tim/Adobe Stock Photos.

Page 64: Vasyl/Adobe Stock Photos, Evan-Amos/Wikimedia Commons, Pavlo Plakhotia/Adobe Stock Photos, Pavlo Plakhotia/Adobe Stock Photos, Pavlo Plakhotia/Adobe Stock Photos, Pavlo Plakhotia/Adobe Stock Photos.

Page 66: Wikimedia Commons, MicroOne/Adobe Stock Photos, geralt/22920 images/Pixabay, blende12/4177 images/Pixabay, Pexels/9146 images/Pixabay, Valiphotos/55 images/Pixabay,

Максим Дрон/Adobe Stock Photos, John Smith/Adobe Stock Photos, Jonathan/Adobe Stock Photos, Maridav/Adobe Stock Photos, Ksi/Adobe Stock Photos, kamerman1960/231 images/ Pixabay.

Page 67: PublicDomainPictures/17904/Pixabay, PJL/Wikimedia, Humpty/Adobe Stock Photos, Paylessimages/Adobe Stock Photos, Raysonho/Wikimedia, Michal Ludwiczak/Adobe Stock Photos, Galyna Andrushko/Adobe Stock Photos, JSirlin/Adobe Stock Photos, LOVE A Stock/Adobe Stock Photos, PublicDomainPictures/17904 images/Pixabay, .S. Air Force photo/Tech. Sgt. Ben Bloker/Wikimedia Commons, lucato/Adobe Stock Photos.

Page 68: Wonderful pictures/Adobe Stock Photos, Justin Hobson /Wikimedia Commons, Сергей Сергей/Adobe Stock Photos, Paylessimages/Adobe Stock Photos, tenrec/Adobe Stock Photos, alexyz3d/Adobe Stock Photos, Veniamin/Adobe Stock Photos, Donald A. Swanson, USGS/Wikimedia Commons, Wikimedia Commons, Ксения Куприянова/Adobe Stock Photos, Andrei Stepanov/Adobe Stock Photos, Maygutyak/Adobe Stock Photos.

Page 69: markusspiske/999 images/Pixabay, blickpixel/1910 images/Pixabay, Martyn Glover/Wikimedia Commons, Leonid Ikan/Adobe Stock Photos.

Page 71: kordi_vahle/977 images/Pixabay, amenohi/Adobe Stock Photos, motivthueringen8/Adobe Stock Photos, Vera Kuttelvaserova/Adobe Stock Photos, Fineart Panorama/Adobe Stock Photos, Cmon/Adobe Stock Photos, Wikimedia Commons, by-studio/Adobe Stock Photos, panosud360/Adobe Stock Photos, Florida Keys--Public Library/Flicker, CJ Cauley/ Pexels, dimitrisvetsikas1969/15719 images/Pixabay.

Page 72: jahmaica/Adobe Stock Photos, Wikimedia Commons, Jim Champion/Wikimedia Commons, Zubro/Wikimedia Commons, Артём Ровенский/Adobe Stock Photos, Nick Collins/ Pexels, Paul Mannix/Wikimedia Commons, Chris Light/Wikimedia Commons, by-studio/Adobe Stock Photos, Simon / 1209 images/Pixabay, Free-Photos/9080 images/Pixabay, Tomo Jesenicnik/Adobe Stock Photos.

Page 73: Immanuel Giel/Wikimedia Commons, Rosino/Wikimedia Commons, zlikovec/Adobe Stock Photos, Ivo62/7 images/Pixabay, DorSteffen/Adobe Stock Photos, Realbrvhrt /Wikimedia Commons, alexyz3d/Adobe Stock Photos, Jonny_Joka/782 images/Pixabay, John Smith/Adobe Stock Photos, doris oberfrank-list/Adobe Stock Photos, 12019/10259 images/Pixabay, Colliefreund / 59 images/Pixabay.

Page 75: KlausHausmann/420/Pixabay, MemoryCatcher/4700/Pixabay, Pixabay/Pexels, jplenio/902/Pixabay, Tama66/1964/Pixabay, chungking/Adobe Stock Photos, exis/43/Pixabay, lino9999/141/Pixabay, trongnguyen/Adobe Stock Photos, dola710/Adobe Stock Photos, MarcelloRabozzi/61 images/Pixabay, Sundry Photography/Adobe Stock Photos.

Page 76: Rosemarie/Adobe Stock Photos, wolterke/Adobe Stock Photos, Fotoluminate LLC/Adobe Stock Photos, 12019/10259/Pixabay, kmiragaya/Adobe Stock Photos, jack-sooksan/Adobe Stock Photos, Eliezer Weishoff/Wikimedia, rachid amrous/Adobe Stock Photos, Taras Vyshnya/Adobe Stock Photos.

Chapter 04

Page 80: eyetronic/Adobe Stock Photos, PhotoKD/Adobe Stock Photos, Alexander Raths/Adobe Stock Photos, dhrdl83/6/Pixabay, petrrgoskov/Adobe Stock Photos, Jag_cz/Adobe Stock Photos, RitaE/2846/Pixabay, New Africa/Adobe Stock Photos, vladteodor/Adobe Stock Photos, michaeljung/Adobe Stock Photos, stormy/Adobe Stock Photos, tilialucida/Adobe Stock Photos.

Page 81: kittyfly/Adobe Stock Photos, Katie Smith/Unsplash.

Page 82: Hihitetlin/Adobe Stock Photos, Dalmatin.o/Adobe Stock Photos, MissesJones/Adobe Stock Photos, Quade/Adobe Stock Photos, Joe Gough/Adobe Stock Photos, u_rt5bpvly/1/Pixabay, lefebvre_jonathan/Adobe Stock Photos, Coprid/Adobe Stock Photos, evgenyb/Adobe Stock Photos, Maurice Metzger/Adobe Stock Photos, guy/Adobe Stock Photos, ange1011/Adobe Stock Photos.

Page 83: Mara Zemgaliete/Adobe Stock Photos, milanchikov/Adobe Stock Photos, smuay/Adobe Stock Photos, M.studio/Adobe Stock Photos, Viktor/Adobe Stock Photos, eNjoy Istyle/Adobe Stock Photos, Alexander Raths/Adobe Stock Photos, Viktor/Adobe Stock Photos, pioneer111/Adobe Stock Photos, ALF photo/Adobe Stock Photos, Viktor/Adobe Stock Photos, milanchikov/Adobe Stock Photos.

Page 84: Mara Zemgaliete/Adobe Stock Photos, ahirao/Adobe Stock Photos, vadimnekhaev_ru/Adobe Stock Photos, ExQuisine/Adobe Stock Photos, Andrey/Adobe Stock Photos, Richard Griffin/Adobe Stock Photos, assja_sav/Adobe Stock Photos, assja_sav/Adobe Stock Photos, assja_sav/Adobe Stock Photos, Pineapple studio/Adobe Stock Photos, Vita/Adobe Stock Photos, JackStock/Adobe Stock Photos.

Page 85: volga1971/Adobe Stock Photos, Bert Folsom/Adobe Stock Photos, Viktor/Adobe Stock Photos, pavel siamionov/Adobe Stock Photos.

Page 86: whitestorm/Adobe Stock Photos, diamant24/Adobe Stock Photos, gitusik/Adobe Stock Photos, kab-vision/Adobe Stock Photos, Marco Mayer/Adobe Stock Photos, akf/Adobe Stock Photos, Patryk Kosmider/Adobe Stock Photos, Gaetan Soupa/Adobe Stock Photos, ExQuisine/Adobe Stock Photos, Bernd Schmidt/Adobe Stock Photos, FOOD-pictures/Adobe Stock Photos, shootdiem/Adobe Stock Photos.

Page 87: Picture Partners/Adobe Stock Photos, Christian Jung/Adobe Stock Photos, robert6666/Adobe Stock Photos, Lsantilli/Adobe Stock Photos, Mara Zemgaliete/Adobe Stock Photos, BlackRiv/66/Pixabay, reshoot/Adobe Stock Photos, reshoot/Adobe Stock Photos, philip kinsey/Adobe Stock Photos, pamela_d_mcadams/Adobe Stock Photos, Moving Moment/Adobe Stock Photos, Maceo/Adobe Stock Photos.

Page 88: Igor Dudchak/Adobe Stock Photos, Lana Langlois/Adobe Stock Photos, L.Bouvier/Adobe Stock Photos, xu_mingxm/1/Pixabay, AnnRos/141/Pixabay, ksena32/Adobe Stock Photos, GSDesign/Adobe Stock Photos, vandycandy/Adobe

Stock Photos, Volodymyr Shevchuk/Adobe Stock Photos, karelnoppe/Adobe Stock Photos, photocrew/Adobe Stock Photos, Oleg Zhukov/Adobe Stock Photos.

Page 89: emmapeel34/Adobe Stock Photos, Alexandr/Adobe Stock Photos, imagemonkey/Adobe Stock Photos, Sergio Martínez/Adobe Stock Photos.

Page 90: exclusive-design/Adobe Stock Photos, Jiri Hera/Adobe Stock Photos, PublicDomainPictures/17902/Pixabay, nino-ninos/Adobe Stock Photos, nito/Adobe Stock Photos, sommai/Adobe Stock Photos, imagineilona/Adobe Stock Photos, mali maeder/Pexels, rdnzl/Adobe Stock Photos, larcobasso/Adobe Stock Photos, ChaoticDesignStudio/Adobe Stock Photos, Iurii Kachkovskyi/Adobe Stock Photos.

Page 91: Iurii Kachkovskyi/Adobe Stock Photos, shibachuu/Adobe Stock Photos, Dionisvera/Adobe Stock Photos, prairie_eye/E+/Getty Images, rdnzl/Adobe Stock Photos, gavran333/Adobe Stock Photos, cabecademarmore/Adobe Stock Photos, Birgit Reitz-Hofmann/Adobe Stock Photos, Anatoly Repin/Adobe Stock Photos, PublicDomainPictures/17904/Pixabay, Momentum Fotograh/Shutterstock.com, shibachuu/Adobe Stock Photos.

Page 92: mariusz_g/Adobe Stock Photos, Buntysmum/4252/Pixabay, hcast/Adobe Stock Photos, Elena Schweitzer/Adobe Stock Photos, DW labs Incorporated/Adobe Stock Photos, Jiri Hera/Adobe Stock Photos, Natika/Adobe Stock Photos, JRP Studio/Adobe Stock Photos, Lev/Adobe Stock Photos, PublicDomainPictures/17904/Pixabay, PublicDomainPictures/17904/Pixabay, Shutterbug75/ 907 images/Pixabay.

Page 93: Dubravko Sorić/Flickr, WikimediaImages/5817/Pixabay, sarahdoow/Adobe Stock Photos, Picture Partners/Adobe Stock Photos, Valentina R./Adobe Stock Photos.

Page 95: eyewave/Adobe Stock Photos, Elena Schweitzer/Adobe Stock Photos, dessuil/2/Pixabay, Lebensmittelfotos/227/Pixabay, kolesnikovserg/Adobe Stock Photos, Elena Schweitzer/Adobe Stock Photos, a_m_radul/Adobe Stock Photos, riccardomotti/Adobe Stock Photos, todja/Adobe Stock Photos, andriigorulko/Adobe Stock Photos, Moving Moment/Adobe Stock Photos, Colin & Linda McKie/Adobe Stock Photos.

Page 96: photocrew/Adobe Stock Photos, osoznaniejizni/Adobe Stock Photos, Stephane Duchateau/Adobe Stock Photos, Moving Moment/Adobe Stock Photos.

Page 97: PublicDomainImages/716/Pixabay, JorgeReynal/15/Pixabay, guy/Adobe Stock Photos, kiboka/Adobe Stock Photos, koosen/Adobe Stock Photos, rockvillephoto/Adobe Stock Photos, unpict/Adobe Stock Photos, blende12/4177/Pixabay, unpict/Adobe Stock Photos, clubfoto/E+/Getty Images, New Africa/Adobe Stock Photos, Rawpixel.com/Adobe Stock Photo.

Page 98: nd700/Adobe Stock Photos, HG Photography/Shutterstock.com, PerfectLinks/13/Pixabay, Tomomarusan/Wikipedia, Alexas_Fotos/21623/Pixabay, Tabeajaichhalt/368/Pixabay, Suzy Hazelwood/Pexels, PublicDomainPictures/17904/Pixabay, Adobe Systems Incorporated, nikkytok/Adobe Stock Photos, Brent Hofacker/Adobe Stock Photos, viennetta14/Adobe Stock Photos.

Page 99: Mara Zemgaliete/Adobe Stock Photos, Seregam/Shutterstock.com, Jiri Hera/Adobe Stock Photos, baibaz/Adobe Stock Photos, M.studio/Adobe Stock Photos, ampFotoStudio.com/Adobe Stock Photos, PublicDomainPictures/17904/Pixabay.

Page 101: alinamd/Adobe Stock Photos, nortongo/Adobe Stock Photos, Tim UR/Adobe Stock Photos, PublicDomainPictures/17904/Pixabay, yvdavid/Adobe Stock Photos, Diana Taliun/Adobe Stock Photos, Tim UR/Adobe Stock Photos, illustrez-vous/Adobe Stock Photos, yvdavid/Adobe Stock Photos, Dean Turner/E+/Getty Images, andersphoto/Adobe Stock Photos, atoss/Adobe Stock Photos.

Page 102: Serhiy Shullye/Adobe Stock Photos, Ian 2010/Shutterstock.com, Adobe Systems Incorporated, baibaz/Adobe Stock Photos, kolesnikovserg/Adobe Stock Photos, Natika/Adobe Stock Photos, Anna Sedneva/Adobe Stock Photos, baibaz/Adobe Stock Photos, Iurii Kachkovskyi/Adobe Stock Photos, kovaleva_ka/Adobe Stock Photos, bestphotostudio/Adobe Stock Photos, Mariusz Blach/Adobe Stock Photos.

Page 103: akamaraqu/Adobe Stock Photos, digieye/Adobe Stock Photos, angelo gilardelli/Shutterstock.com, alexlukin/

Adobe Stock Photos, Serhiy Shullye/Adobe Stock Photos, varintorn/42/Pixabay, alexlukin/Adobe Stock Photos, krasyuk/Adobe Stock Photos, mates/Adobe Stock Photos, valery121283/Adobe Stock Photos, Tim UR/Adobe Stock Photos.

Page 105: Robyn Mackenzie/Shutterstock.com, Adobe Systems Incorporated, baibaz/Adobe Stock Photos, Mara Zemgaliete/Adobe Stock Photos, Magone/iStock/Getty Images, Picture Partners/Adobe Stock Photos, Robyn Mackenzie/iStock/Getty Images, Picture Partners/Adobe Stock Photos, Brad Pict/Adobe Stock Photos, Joe Gough/Adobe Stock Photos, Elena Schweitzer/Shutterstock.com, Buecherwurm_65/59/Pixabay.

Page 106: eqroy/Adobe Stock Photos, Dionisvera/Shutterstock.com, zcy/Adobe Stock Photos, kolesnikovserg/Adobe Stock Photos, Altnet/25/Pixabay, nipaporn/Adobe Stock Photos, Jill Fromer/iStock/Getty Images, Artem Gorohov/Adobe Stock Photos, eyewave/Adobe Stock Photos, osoznaniejizni/Adobe Stock Photos, Popova Olga/Adobe Stock Photos, Sasa Komlen/Adobe Stock Photos.

Page 107: David Bishop Inc./Stockbyte/Getty Images, dabok2014/10 images/Pixabay, Johnstocker/10 images/Pixabay, Mara Zemgaliete/Adobe Stock Photos, Valentyn Volkov/Shutterstock.com, iprachenko/Adobe Stock Photos, Jatinder Kumar/Adobe Stock Photos, Elena Schweitzer/Adobe Stock Photos, Picture Partners/Adobe Stock Photos, Anson/Adobe Stock Photos, volff/Adobe Stock Photos.

Page 109: Viktor/Adobe Stock Photos, Moving Moment/Adobe Stock Photos, xamtiw/Adobe Stock Photos, Roman Ivaschenko/Adobe Stock Photos, karandaev/Adobe Stock Photos, unpict/Adobe Stock Photos, Kalavati/Adobe Stock Photos, koosen/Adobe Stock Photos, Vasily/Adobe Stock Photos, janvier/Adobe Stock Photos, Gresei/Adobe Stock Photos, Scisetti Alfio/Adobe Stock Photos.

Page 110: womue/Adobe Stock Photos, oleh11/Adobe Stock Photos, nd700/Adobe Stock Photos, Dionisvera/Adobe Stock Photos, robert6666/Adobe Stock Photos, Natika/Adobe Stock Photos, nazarovsergey/Adobe Stock Photos, Nataly-Nete/Adobe Stock Photos, Jörg Rautenberg/Adobe Stock Photos, andriigorulko/Adobe Stock Photos, Роман Фернаті/Adobe Stock Photos, seramoje/Adobe Stock Photos.

Page 111: Scisetti Alfio/Adobe Stock Photos, duncanandison/ Adobe Stock Photos, niteenrk/Adobe Stock Photos, Diana Taliun/Adobe Stock Photos, Svetlana Kuznetsova/Adobe Stock Photos, luissybuster/Adobe Stock Photos, Angel Simon/ Adobe Stock Photos, constantinos/Adobe Stock Photos, Superheang168/Adobe Stock Photos, Viktor/Adobe Stock Photos, lathuric/iStock/Getty Images, Valentina R./Adobe Stock Photos.

Page 112: margo555/Adobe Stock Photos, Elena Odareeva/ Adobe Stock Photos, wealthy lady/Adobe Stock Photos, kaiskynet/Adobe Stock Photos.

Page 113: Pexels, goodluz/Adobe Stock Photos, Studio Romantic/Adobe Stock, Margarita Cherniak/Unsplash, arsa35/Adobe Stock Photos, WavebreakMediaMicro/Adobe Stock Photos, EdNurg/Adobe Stock Photos, annbozhko/Adobe Stock Photos, Syda Productions/Adobe Stock Photos, islandworks/333 images/Pixabay, Magdalena Bujak/Adobe Stock Photos, exclusive-design/Adobe Stock Photos.

Page 114: Thamarai/Adobe Stock Photos, Brian Jackson/Adobe Stock Photos, borisimple/Adobe Stock Photos, Andrey Popov/ Adobe Stock Photos, vinnstock/Adobe Stock Photos, Kevin Curtis/Unsplash, mangpor2004/Adobe Stock Photos, fizkes/Adobe Stock Photos.

Page 116: sveta/Adobe Stock Photos, uckyo/Adobe Stock Photos, Wichit S/Adobe Stock Photos, 8664447/60 images/Pixabay, annanes13/124 images/Pixabay, tookapic/1076 images/ Pixabay, Silberfuchs/301 images/Pixabay, nataliazakharova/ Adobe Stock Photos, Silberfuchs/Pixabay, Silberfuchs/301 images/Pixabay, Silberfuchs/301 images/Pixabay, Pixabay.

Page 117: Yuri_B/132 images/Pixabay, Viktor/Adobe Stock Photos, Coprid/Adobe Stock Photos, cloud7days/Adobe Stock Photos, Artur Nyk/Adobe Stock Photos, Gresei/Adobe Stock Photos, Surbucca/Shutterstock.com, maciej326/150 images/ Pixabay, Alexstar/Adobe Stock Photos, siriratsavett/Shutterstock.com, karandaev/Adobe Stock Photos.

Page 119: dusk/Adobe Stock Photos, ake1150/Adobe Stock Photos, beataaldridge/Adobe Stock Photos, chandlervid85/Adobe Stock Photos, Intuitivmedia/31 images/Pixabay, bbivirys/Adobe Stock Photos, annapustynnikova/Adobe Stock Photos, Brent Hofacker/Adobe Stock Photos, helenedevun/Adobe Stock Photos, MissesJones/Adobe Stock Photos, Juanmonino/Getty Images, thodonal/Adobe Stock Photos.

Page 120: M.studio/Adobe Stock Photos, Claude Calcagno/Adobe Stock Photos, Marc Rigaud/Adobe Stock Photos, George Dolgikh/Adobe Stock Photos, Sławomir Fajer/Adobe Stock Photos, SOLLUB/Adobe Stock Photos, Наталья Майорова/Adobe Stock Photos, Bart/Adobe Stock Photos, M.studio/Adobe Stock Photos, Magdalena Bujak/Adobe Stock Photos, Magalice/Adobe Stock Photos, beats_/Adobe Stock Photos.

Page 121: vm2002/Adobe Stock Photos, Nelea Reazanteva/Adobe Stock Photos, Liudmyla/Adobe Stock Photos, Georges/Adobe Stock Photos, M.studio/Adobe Stock Photos, t.sableaux/Adobe Stock Photos, M.studio/Adobe Stock Photos, Studio Gi/Adobe Stock Photos, Роман Самсонов/Adobe Stock Photos, N.Van Doninck/Adobe Stock Photos, Fanfo/Adobe Stock Photos, rainbow33/Adobe Stock Photos.

Page 122: daumy/Adobe Stock Photos, FOOD-micro/Adobe Stock Photos, Fanfo/Adobe Stock Photos, zakiroff/Adobe Stock Photos.

Page 124: William Berry/Adobe Stock Photos, veleri_kz/Adobe Stock Photos, freshidea/Adobe Stock Photos, martialred/Adobe Stock Photos, Aluxum/Shutterstock.com, Tatutati/384 images/Pixabay, calypso77/Adobe Stock Photos, chutima/Adobe Stock Photos, rewind/31 images/Pixabay, modisketch/Adobe Stock Photos, Balint Radu/Adobe Stock Photos, san_ta/Adobe Stock Photos.

Page 126: Rawpixel.com/Adobe Stock Photos, Evgeny Dubinchuk/Adobe Stock Photos, picsfive/Adobe Stock Photos, sum41/Adobe Stock Photos, Maximo Sanz/Adobe Stock Photos, Alexas_Fotos/21623 images/Pixabay, dimakp/Adobe Stock Photos, rudisetiawan/Adobe Stock Photos, frogstyle/Adobe Stock Photos, M.studio/Adobe Stock Photos, balt/5 images/Pixabay, PhotoMIX-Company/372 images/Pixabay.

Page 127: phive2015/Adobe Stock Photos, ChaoticDesignStudio/Adobe Stock Photos, M.studio/Adobe Stock Photos, ArtemSam/Adobe Stock Photos, Gresei/Adobe Stock Photos, gielmichal/Adobe Stock Photos, M.studio/Adobe Stock Photos, Jenifoto/Adobe Stock Photos, maryviolet/Adobe Stock Photos, Elena Elisseeva/Shutterstock.com, Scanrail/Adobe Stock Photos, Daria-Yakovleva/145 images/Pixabay.

Page 128: Korta/Adobe Stock Photos, Yeti Studio/Adobe Stock Photos.

Page 129: goir/Adobe Stock Photos, Chursina Viktoriia/Shutterstock.com, Mariyana M/Adobe Stock Photos, baibaz/Adobe Stock Photos, Luminis/Adobe Stock Photos, hansgeel/Adobe Stock Photos, Nigel Monckton/Adobe Stock Photos, Julián Rovagnati/Adobe Stock Photos, Sea Wave/Adobe Stock Photos, stevepb/561 images, Семен Саливанчук/Adobe Stock Photos, by-studio/Adobe Stock Photos.

Page 130: wbe1951/109 images/Pixabay, Dzha/Adobe Stock Photos, Coprid/Adobe Stock Photos, monticellllo/Adobe Stock Photos, maxsol7/Adobe Stock Photos, Dmitry Ersler/Adobe Stock Photos, baibaz/Adobe Stock Photos.

Chapter 05

Page 134: Daniel Thomas/Unsplash, ArchiVIZ/Adobe Stock Photos, Vitaliy Hrabar/Adobe Stock Photos, Kalim/Adobe Stock Photos, OceanProd/Adobe Stock Photos, Rawf8/Adobe Stock Photos, Falkenpost/169 images/Pixabay, davidlee770924/10 images/Pixabay, Soloviova Liudmyla/Adobe Stock Photos, Helena Lopes/Pexels, Sharpshot/Adobe Stock Photos, 영인 진/Adobe Stock Photos.

Page 135: Kaspars Grinvalds/Adobe Stock Photos, LIGHTFIELD STUDIOS/Adobe Stock Photos, DragonImages/Adobe Stock Photos, VAKSMANV/Adobe Stock Photos, Robert Kneschke/Adobe Stock Photos, Atstock Productions/Adobe Stock Photos, DragonImages/Adobe Stock Photos, ChenPG/Adobe Stock Photos, Monkey Business/Adobe Stock Photos, Steven Pepple/Adobe Stock Photos, Africa Studio/Adobe Stock Photos, LIGHTFIELD STUDIOS/Adobe Stock Photos.

Page 136: rh2010/Adobe Stock Photos, Michelleraponi/3532 images/Pixabay, solskin/12 images/Pixabay, sepy/Adobe Stock Photos, alexandre zveiger/Adobe Stock Photos, Izhak Agency/Unsplash, Michelleraponi/3532 images/Pixabay, Barun Ghosh/Unsplash, epicioci/219 images/Pixabay, Pavel Losevsky/Adobe Stock Photos, monicore/1146 images/Pixabay, abramsdesign/Adobe Stock Photos.

Page 137: olly/Adobe Stock Photos, dglimages/Adobe Stock Photos, ivabalk/2260/Pixabay, nattul/Adobe Stock Photos, Elnur/Adobe Stock Photos, Paul Vinten/Adobe Stock Photos, dit26978/Adobe Stock Photos, Anna Vovk/Adobe Stock Photos, meailleluc.com/Adobe Stock Photos, New Africa/Adobe Stock Photos, Mel Poole/Unsplash, didecs/Adobe Stock Photos.

Page 138: ErikaWittlieb/Pixabay, ludmilafoto/Adobe Stock Photos, ONNE Beauty/Unsplash, navintar/Adobe Stock Photos, Viktor Forgacs/Unsplash, yuichi2k/Adobe Stock Photos, gpointstudio/Adobe Stock Photos, thayra83/Adobe Stock Photos, Africa Studio/Adobe Stock Photos, nd700/Adobe Stock Photos, Juli Kosolapova/Unsplash, Max Vakhtbovych/Pexels.

Page 139: leopoldboettcher/62/Pixabay, michaklootwijk/Adobe Stock Photos, stockcrafter/Adobe Stock Photos, Kenishirotie/Adobe Stock Photos, Urric/Adobe Stock Photos, Prostock-studio/Adobe Stock Photos, mario beauregard/Adobe Stock Photos, New Africa/Adobe Stock Photos, Andrey Popov/Adobe Stock Photos, polack/Adobe Stock Photos, Kalim/Adobe Stock Photos, Kzenon/Adobe Stock Photos.

Page 140: auremar/Adobe Stock Photos, Andrey Popov/Adobe Stock Photos, elnariz/Adobe Stock Photos, Halfpoint/Adobe Stock Photos, AntonioDiaz/Adobe Stock Photos, REDPIXEL/Adobe Stock Photos, MclittleStock/Adobe Stock Photos, Elnur/Adobe Stock Photos, alotofpeople/Adobe Stock Photos.

Page 143: benschonewille/Adobe Stock Photos, sarangib/4544 images/Pixabay, Daxiao Productions/Adobe Stock Photos, exclusive-design/Adobe Stock Photos, Yay Images/Adobe Stock Photos, Ree/Adobe Stock Photos, bmak/Adobe Stock Photos, auremar/Adobe Stock Photos, Mathia/Adobe Stock Photos, Michael Pettigrew/Adobe Stock Photos.

Page 145: pab_map/Adobe Stock Photos, JackF/Adobe Stock Photos, radiokafka/Adobe Stock Photos, radiokafka/Adobe Stock Photos, Alexey Lesik/Adobe Stock Photos, Довидович Михаил/Adobe Stock Photos, carles/Adobe Stock Photos, JackF/Adobe Stock Photos, auremar/Adobe Stock Photos, Pavel Losevsky/Adobe Stock Photos, adisa/Adobe Stock Photos, Goffkein/Adobe Stock Photos.

Page 146: iushakovsky/Adobe Stock Photos, gavran333/Adobe Stock Photos, Vitaly Sova/Adobe Stock Photos.

Page 147: gpointstudio/Adobe Stock Photos, natalia_maroz/Adobe Stock Photos, Flashon Studio/Shutterstock.com, Harvey Hudson/Adobe Stock Photos, robepco/Adobe Stock Photos, Siegfried Schnepf/Adobe Stock Photos, Deyan Georgiev/Adobe Stock Photos, Roman Babakin/Adobe Stock Photos, Shutter2U/Adobe Stock Photos, zavgsg/Adobe Stock Photos, John Kasawa/Adobe Stock Photos, paul prescott/Adobe Stock Photos.

Page 148: kornnphoto/Adobe Stock Photos, PJ_JoE/Adobe Stock Photos, latite06/Adobe Stock Photos, Satjawat/Adobe Stock Photos, Galyna Andrushko/Adobe Stock Photos, WikimediaImages/5817/Pixabay, Vaceslav Romanov/Adobe Stock Photos, ChiccoDodiFC/Adobe Stock Photos, Kryuchka Yaroslav/Adobe Stock Photos, Sergey Ryzhov/Adobe Stock Photos, arthito/Adobe Stock Photos, Pam Walker/Adobe Stock Photos.

Page 149: BillionPhotos.com/Adobe Stock Photos, myphotobank.com.au/Adobe Stock Photos, hanohiki/Adobe Stock Photos, tarasov_vl/Adobe Stock Photos, Coprid/Adobe Stock Photos, abramsdesign/Adobe Stock Photos, CLShebley/Adobe Stock Photos, Veniamin Kraskov/Adobe Stock Photos, Prostock-studio/Adobe Stock Photos, zcy/Adobe Stock Photos, anela47/Adobe Stock Photos, Peter de Kievith/Adobe Stock Photos.

Page 150: leekris/Adobe Stock Photos, exclusive-design/Adobe Stock Photos, Dmitry Naumov/Adobe Stock Photos, Halfpoint/Adobe Stock Photos, Sergey/Adobe Stock Photos, Scottie/Adobe Stock Photos, micromonkey/Adobe Stock Photos, gilitukha/Adobe Stock Photos.

Page 152: Olivier Le Moal/Adobe Stock Photos, coralimages/Adobe Stock Photos, bmak/Adobe Stock Photos, bmak/Adobe Stock Photos, victor zastol'skiy/Adobe Stock Photos, OceanProd/Adobe Stock Photos, terovesalainen/Adobe Stock Photos, hakinmhan/Adobe Stock Photos, Alexey Shkitenkov/Adobe Stock Photos, Daxiao Productions/Adobe Stock Photos, Daxiao Productions/Adobe Stock Photos, Photographee.eu/Adobe Stock Photos.

Page 153: Kitaeva Tatiana/Shutterstock.com, sunny_bunny/Adobe Stock Photos, tejasp/3/Pixabay, Jacob Lund/Adobe Stock Photos, coralimages/Adobe Stock Photos, sean824/Adobe Stock Photos, Naypong Studio/Adobe Stock Photos, M.studio/Adobe Stock Photos, Victor/Adobe Stock Photos, oktay/Adobe Stock Photos, Zigmar Stein/Adobe Stock Photos, xixinxing/Adobe Stock Photos.

Page 154: petert2/Adobe Stock Photos, 昊 周/Adobe Stock Photos, eriyalim/Adobe Stock Photos, bernardbodo/Adobe Stock Photos, zimmytws/Adobe Stock Photos, mipan/Adobe Stock Photos, Jeff Whyte/Adobe Stock Photos, rilueda/Adobe Stock Photos, FeellFree/Shutterstock.com, leopoldboettcher/62/Pixabay, alexnikit/Adobe Stock Photos, Finmiki/Adobe Stock Photos.

Page 155: Carol A Hudson/Adobe Stock Photos, faraktinov/Adobe Stock Photos, Kenishirotie/Adobe Stock Photos, Pixel-Shot/Adobe Stock Photos, ILYA AKINSHIN/Adobe Stock Photos, NDABCREATIVITY/Adobe Stock Photos, Thammasiri/Adobe Stock Photos, maykal/Adobe Stock Photos, Siam/Adobe Stock Photos, merly69/Adobe Stock Photos, Flamingo Images/Adobe Stock Photos, oktay/Adobe Stock Photos.

Page 156: KKulikov/Shutterstock.com, VTT Studio/Adobe Stock Photos.

Page 157: dglimages/Adobe Stock Photos, ivabalk/2260/Pixabay, Johnny Lye/Adobe Stock Photos, ArchiVIZ/Adobe Stock Photos, photopixel/Adobe Stock Photos, terng99/Adobe Stock Photos, canbedone/Adobe Stock Photos, nuanton/Adobe Stock Photos, John Kasawa/Adobe Stock Photos, poligonchik/Adobe Stock Photos, Photographee.eu/Adobe Stock Photos, Monteleone/Adobe Stock Photos.

Page 159: Photographee.eu/Adobe Stock Photos, dimamoroz/Adobe Stock Photos, sveta/Adobe Stock Photos, Anthony Paz/Adobe Stock Photos, didecs/Adobe Stock Photos, Photographee.eu/Adobe Stock Photos, kazoka303030/Adobe Stock Photos, sveta/Adobe Stock Photos, freestyle_images/Adobe Stock Photos, juriskraulis/Adobe Stock Photos, poplasen/ Adobe Stock Photos, poligonchik/Adobe Stock Photos.

Page 160: LIGHTFIELD STUDIOS/Adobe Stock Photos, Oleksandr/Adobe Stock Photos, Pexels/9145/Pixabay, Mushy/ Adobe Stock Photos, Vera/Adobe Stock Photos, tobago77/ Adobe Stock Photos, brizmaker/Adobe Stock Photos, gupi/ Adobe Stock Photos, Volodymyr Shcerbak/Adobe Stock Photos, koll/Shutterstock.com, New Africa/Adobe Stock Photos, Photographee.eu/Adobe Stock Photos.

Page 161: Popova Olga/Adobe Stock Photos, PhotoKD/Adobe Stock Photos, Pixel-Shot/Adobe Stock Photos, whyframeshot/ Adobe Stock Photos, penkanya/Adobe Stock Photos, Suzi/ Adobe Stock Photos, gielmichal/Shutterstock.com, sirtravelalot/Shutterstock.com, Bits and Splits/Adobe Stock Photos, Rob hyrons/Adobe Stock Photos, Momentmal/1437/Pixabay, s-ts/ Shutterstock.com.

Page 162: lenets_tan/Adobe Stock Photos, annebel146/Adobe Stock Photos.

Page 163: moodboard/Adobe Stock Photos, ILYA AKINSHIN/ Adobe Stock Photos, navintar/Adobe Stock Photos, PlusONE/ Shutterstock/Getty Images, hues/Adobe Stock Photos, picsfive/Adobe Stock Photos, Jason/Adobe Stock Photos, bakhtiar irwandie/EyeEm/Adobe Stock Photos, prescott09/Adobe Stock Photos, Rinku/Adobe Stock Photos, Ivonne Wierink/Adobe Stock Photos, esoxx/Adobe Stock Photos.

Page 164: maykal/Adobe Stock Photos, gpointstudio/Adobe Stock Photos, No attribution required, milanmarkovic78/ Adobe Stock Photos, succo/964 images/Pixabay, Pixel-Shot/ Adobe Stock Photos, Maksym Yemelyanov/Adobe Stock Photos, ewapee/Adobe Stock Photos, chatchawan/Adobe Stock Photos, Kuzmick/Adobe Stock Photos, timothyh/Adobe Stock Photos, NDABCREATIVITY/Adobe Stock Photos.

Page 165: EuToch/Adobe Stock Photos, Olha/Adobe Stock Photos, Miyuki Satake/Adobe Stock Photos, FeellFree/Shutterstock.com, Prostock-studio/Adobe Stock Photos, New Africa/Adobe Stock Photos, juniart/Adobe Stock Photos, Tomislav/Adobe Stock Photos, bruce mars/Unsplash, rh2010/Adobe Stock Photos, Lars Zahner/Adobe Stock Photos, jayzynism/Adobe Stock Photos.

Page 166: Artem/Adobe Stock Photos, luckybusiness/Adobe Stock Photos.

Page 167: Panama/Adobe Stock Photos, pumpnoi/Adobe Stock Photos, pumpnoi/Adobe Stock Photos, Bits and Splits/Adobe Stock Photos, Voyagerix/Adobe Stock Photos, sebra/Adobe Stock, Nicolas Gregor/Adobe Stock Photos, Marina Lohrbach/Adobe Stock Photos, carol_anne/Adobe Stock Photos, Ilja/Adobe Stock Photos, Andrzej Tokarski/Adobe Stock Photos, Pixel-Shot/Adobe Stock Photos.

Chapter 06

Page 170: visart/Adobe Stock Photos, ractapopulous/2998 images/Pixabay, djmilic/Adobe Stock Photos, chrisdorney/Adobe Stock Photos, dotsent/Adobe Stock Photos, koya979/Adobe Stock Photos, nowyn/Adobe Stock Photos, detailfoto/Adobe Stock Photos, Photobeps/Adobe Stock Photos, vadim yerofeyev/Adobe Stock Photos, Miguel Á.Padriñán/Pexels, Clker-Free-Vector-Images/29565 images/Pixabay.

Page 171: martincp/Adobe Stock Photos, lukasz_kochanek/Adobe Stock Photos, Robert Herhold/Adobe Stock Photos, stavros mantzaris/EyeEm/Adobe Stock Photos, martincp/Adobe Stock Photos, martincp/Adobe Stock Photos, papparaffie/Adobe Stock Photos, sandra scheumann/EyeEm/Adobe Stock Photos, Lance Bellers/Adobe Stock Photos, paul tune/EyeEm/Adobe Stock Photos, papparaffie/Adobe Stock Photos, nowyn/Adobe Stock Photos.

Page 172: TanteTati/1189 images/Pixabay, Poliorketes/Adobe Stock Photos, Atarythm / 22 images, Magda Ehlers/Pexels, Srdjan/Adobe Stock Photos, djumandji/Adobe Stock Photos, satura_/Adobe Stock Photos, ChiccoDodiFC/Adobe Stock Photos, Dmytro Synelnychenko/Adobe Stock Photos, michaklootwijk/Adobe Stock Photos, kegfire/Adobe Stock Photos, gazanfer/Adobe Stock.

Page 173: kostiuchenko/Adobe Stock Photos, Davein/Adobe Stock Photos, Evgeny/Adobe Stock Photos, Rubel/Adobe Stock Photos, alexlmx/Adobe Stock Photos, zavgsg/Adobe Stock Photos, MarekPhotoDesign.com/Adobe Stock Photos, Mastr/Adobe Stock Photos, LUke1138/iStock/Getty Images, Richard Johnson/Adobe Stock Photos, trongnguyen/Adobe Stock Photos, xy/Adobe Stock Photos.

Page 174: Pcess609/Adobe Stock Photos, Rawf8/Adobe Stock Photos, sunday_morning/Adobe Stock Photos, Boggy/Adobe Stock Photos, rh2010/Adobe Stock Photos, H_Ko/Adobe Stock Photos, cherylvb/Adobe Stock Photos.

Page 176: Fotodesign Fast/Adobe Stock Photos, IEVTIEIEV OLEKSANDR/Adobe Stock Photos, Andrey_Lobachev/Adobe Stock Photos, bjoerno/Adobe Stock Photos, Carlos Pernalete Tua/Pexels, jvinasd/Adobe Stock Photos, Vladimir Mucibabic/Adobe Stock Photos.

Page 177: thodonal/Adobe Stock Photos, mehaniq41/Adobe Stock Photos, spalaukou/Adobe Stock Photos.

Page 178: Brian Jackson/Adobe Stock Photos, Syda Productions/Adobe Stock Photos, sabelskaya/Adobe Stock Photos, eugenie_korni/Adobe Stock Photos, thawornnurak/Adobe Stock Photos, robynmac/Adobe Stock Photos, PaulPaladin/Adobe Stock Photos, o_a/Adobe Stock Photos, Rawpixel.com/Adobe Stock Photos, GAlexS/Adobe Stock Photos.

Page 179: wedninth/Adobe Stock Photos, DGTL Graphics sro/Adobe Stock Photos, auremar/Adobe Stock Photos, elnariz/Adobe Stock Photos, cunaplus/Adobe Stock Photos, vinnstock/Adobe Stock Photos, Pixel-Shot/Adobe Stock Photos, Volodymyr Shevchuk/Adobe Stock Photos, torsak/Adobe Stock Photos, Pixel-Shot/Adobe Stock Photos, RomixImage/Adobe Stock Photos, fizkes/Adobe Stock Photos.

Page 180: Maksym Yemelyanov/Adobe Stock Photos, ungvar/Adobe Stock Photos, U. J. Alexander/Adobe Stock Photos, daviles/Adobe Stock Photos, alswart/Adobe Stock Photos, gearstd/Adobe Stock Photos, Kittiwat/Adobe Stock Photos, Sashkin/Adobe Stock Photos, alswart/Adobe Stock Photos, photobyphotoboy/Adobe Stock Photos.

Page 183: Kirk Fisher/Adobe Stock Photos, paulaphoto/Adobe Stock Photos, Balate Dorin/Adobe Stock Photos, Rawpixel.com/ Adobe Stock Photos, vejaa/Adobe Stock Photos, malexeum/ Adobe Stock Photos, Photocreo Bednarek/Adobe Stock Photos, saiko3p/Adobe Stock Photos, Monkey Business/Adobe Stock Photos, Nejron Photo/Adobe Stock Photos, THINK b/ Adobe Stock Photos, Mihail/Adobe Stock Photos.

Page 184: JackF/Adobe Stock Photos, BlueOrange Studio/Adobe Stock Photos, rh2010/Adobe Stock Photos, Sharif_Whitebear/ Adobe Stock Photos, Tyler Olson/Adobe Stock Photos, Kondor83/Adobe Stock Photos, Kondor83/Adobe Stock Photos, highwaystarz/Adobe Stock Photos, David Pereiras/Adobe Stock Photos, Jacob Lund/Adobe Stock Photos, hedgehog94/ Adobe Stock Photos, monregard/Adobe Stock Photos.

Page 185: Elena Kharichkina/Adobe Stock Photos, Gorodenkoff/Adobe Stock Photos, DragonImages/Adobe Stock Photos, olly/Adobe Stock Photos, jalisko/Adobe Stock Photos, sergantstar/Adobe Stock Photos, paulien tabak/EyeEm/Adobe Stock Photos, Rostislav Sedlacek/Adobe Stock Photos, JackF/Adobe Stock Photos, Maridav/Adobe Stock Photos, Spiroview Inc./ Adobe Stock Photos, Nomad_Soul/Adobe Stock Photos.

Page 186: fascinadora/Adobe Stock Photos, JackF/Adobe Stock Photos, Aisyaqilumar/Adobe Stock Photos, moodboard/Adobe Stock Photos, Elnur/Adobe Stock Photos, Anton Gvozdikov/ Adobe Stock Photos, Tyler Olson/Adobe Stock Photos, JackF/ Adobe Stock Photos, JackF/Adobe Stock Photos, moodboard/ Adobe Stock Photos, hedgehog94/Adobe Stock Photos, Robert Kneschke/Adobe Stock Photos.

Page 187: Viacheslav Iakobchuk/Adobe Stock Photos, bernardbodo/Adobe Stock Photos.

Page 188: Ljupco Smokovski/Adobe Stock Photos, murattellioglu/Adobe Stock Photos, viperagp/Adobe Stock Photos, Corona Borealis/Adobe Stock Photos, Sashkin/Adobe Stock Photos, Luis Angel Garcia/Adobe Stock Photos, mipan/Adobe Stock Photos, .shock/Adobe Stock Photos, diego cervo/Adobe Stock Photos, anaumenko/Adobe Stock Photos, Sergey Ryzhov/ Adobe Stock Photos, PigS/Adobe Stock Photos.

Page 189: Chayanon/Adobe Stock Photos, v74/Adobe Stock Photos, WavebreakMediaMicro/Adobe Stock Photos, Monkey Business/Adobe Stock Photos, phonlamaiphoto/Adobe Stock Photos, Perytskyy/Adobe Stock Photos, Tada Images/Adobe Stock Photos, BillionPhotos.com/Adobe Stock Photos.

Page 191: sosiukin/Adobe Stock Photos, Halfpoint/Adobe Stock Photos, Andris/Adobe Stock Photos, monus_jr8/Adobe Stock Photos, New Africa/Adobe Stock Photos, Marek Mnich/ Adobe Stock Photos, ronstik/Adobe Stock Photos, Africa Studio/Adobe Stock Photos, pressmaster/Adobe Stock Photos.

Page 193: swisshippo/Adobe Stock Photos, Monkey Business/ Adobe Stock Photos, Odua Images/Adobe Stock Photos, Daisy Daisy/Adobe Stock Photos, NorGal/Adobe Stock Photos, Vyacheslav Plyasenko/Adobe Stock Photos, c_atta/Adobe Stock Photos, Andrey Cherkasov/Adobe Stock Photos, geografika/Adobe Stock Photos, chamillew/Adobe Stock Photos, tashka2000/Adobe Stock Photos, tashka2000/Adobe Stock Photos.

Page 194: mavoimages/Adobe Stock Photos, bizoo_n/Adobe Stock Photos, stivog/Adobe Stock Photos, New Africa/Adobe Stock Photos, Monstar Studio/Adobe Stock Photos, Pixel-Shot/ Adobe Stock Photos, Diana Taliun/Adobe Stock Photos, Kybele/Adobe Stock Photos, katyamaximenko/Adobe Stock Photos, Jeff/Adobe Stock Photos, eileen10/Adobe Stock Photos, Ermolaev Alexandr/Adobe Stock Photos.

Page 195: Fxquadro/Adobe Stock Photos, S.Külcü/Adobe Stock Photos, HappyAlex/Adobe Stock Photos, fotofrol/Adobe Stock Photos, Robert Przybysz/Adobe Stock Photos, phoderstock/ Adobe Stock Photos, W PRODUCTION/Adobe Stock Photos, Виталий Сова/Adobe Stock Photos, pressmaster/Adobe Stock Photos, Belish/Adobe Stock Photos, AntonioDiaz/Adobe Stock Photos, arostynov/Adobe Stock Photos.

Page 196: jurra8/Adobe Stock Photos, Florin/Adobe Stock Photos, ikonoklast_hh/Adobe Stock Photos.

Page 197: Africa Studio/Adobe Stock Photos, iroto123/Adobe Stock Photos, dglavinova/Adobe Stock Photos, Adobe Systems Incorporated, YY apartment/Adobe Stock Photos, evgenij918/Adobe Stock Photos, yurchello108/Adobe Stock Photos, sumire8/Adobe Stock Photos, Михаил Александров/Adobe Stock Photos, Rawpixel.com/Adobe Stock, Dmitriy Syechin/Adobe Stock Photos, arts/Adobe Stock Photos.

Page 198: wabeno/Adobe Stock Photos, RUZANNA ARUTYUNYAN/Adobe Stock Photos, michaeljung/Adobe Stock Photos, zcy/Adobe Stock Photos, nito/Adobe Stock Photos, Alexandra_K/Adobe Stock Photos, eightstock/Adobe Stock Photos, srki66/Adobe Stock Photos, chamillew/Adobe Stock Photos, thodonal/Adobe Stock Photos, Irina Rogova/Adobe Stock Photos, Lidiya/Adobe Stock Photos.

Page 199: Khvost/Adobe Stock Photos, DenisProduction.com/Adobe Stock Photos, Anatoliy Sadovskiy/Adobe Stock Photos, Tarzhanova/Adobe Stock Photos, Alexandra_K/Adobe Stock Photos, Lidiya/Adobe Stock Photos, Valentin/Adobe Stock Photos, New Africa/Adobe Stock Photos, Pixel-Shot/Adobe Stock Photos, Thiti/Adobe Stock Photos, butus/Adobe Stock Photos, severija/Adobe Stock Photos.

Page 200: KariDesign/Adobe Stock Photos, Drobot Dean/Adobe Stock Photos, Khvost/Adobe Stock Photos, the_lightwriter/Adobe Stock Photos, Valentin/Adobe Stock Photos, serbogachuk/Adobe Stock Photos, markasia/Adobe Stock Photos, zyryanova/Adobe Stock Photos, dpullman/Adobe Stock Photos, Kayros Studio/Adobe Stock Photos, aimy27feb/Adobe Stock Photos, ludmilafoto/Adobe Stock Photos.

Page 201: ksena32/Adobe Stock Photos, Kaspars Grinvalds/Adobe Stock Photos, Africa Studio/Adobe Stock Photos, Tarzhanova/Adobe Stock Photos, Alexandra_K/Adobe Stock Photos, Elena Stepanova/Adobe Stock Photos, Tarzhanova/Adobe Stock Photos, Restyler/Adobe Stock Photos, ksena32/Adobe Stock Photos, BortN66/Adobe Stock Photos, Alena Ozerova/Adobe Stock Photos, rodjulian/Adobe Stock Photos.

Page 202: Peter Atkins/Adobe Stock Photos, Peter Atkins/Adobe Stock Photos, romankosolapov/Adobe Stock Photos, ArenaCreative/Adobe Stock Photos, likstudio/Adobe Stock Photos, severija/Adobe Stock Photos, vermontalm/Adobe Stock Photos, Peter Hermes Furian/Adobe Stock Photos, ganzia/Adobe Stock Photos, MikeBiTa/Adobe Stock Photos, Елизавета Коробкова/Adobe Stock Photos, Delphotostock/Adobe Stock Photos.

Page 203: Africa Studio/Adobe Stock Photos, VadimGuzhva/Adobe Stock Photos, diignat/Adobe Stock Photos, Friends Stock/Adobe Stock Photos, Prostock-studio/Adobe Stock Photos, Prostock-studio/Adobe Stock Photos, Monkey Business/Adobe Stock Photos, Monkey Business/Adobe Stock Photos, Kana Design Image/Adobe Stock Photos, Ljupco Smokovski/Adobe Stock Photos, tuayai/Adobe Stock Photos, Ilike/Adobe Stock Photos.

Page 204: Africa Studio/Adobe Stock Photos, blackday/Adobe Stock Photos, blackday/Adobe Stock Photos, Axel Bueckert/Adobe Stock Photos, petert2/Adobe Stock Photos, Andrey Popov/Adobe Stock Photos.

Page 205: cabecademarmore/Adobe Stock Photos, Popova Olga/Adobe Stock Photos, nata777_7/Adobe Stock Photos, luckybusiness/Adobe Stock Photos, Dmitriy Golbay/Adobe Stock Photos, Kybele/Adobe Stock Photos, uwimages/Adobe Stock Photos, New Africa/Adobe Stock Photos, pioneer111/Adobe Stock Photos, sergign/Adobe Stock Photos, Vlad/Adobe Stock Photos, Vlad/Adobe Stock Photos.

Page 206: martina87/Adobe Stock Photos, pixelrobot/Adobe Stock Photos, tatomm/Adobe Stock Photos, shaiith/Adobe Stock Photos, Chepko Danil/Adobe Stock Photos, Valerii Zan/Adobe Stock Photos, nastasenko/Adobe Stock Photos, roman_baiadin/Adobe Stock Photos, milosljubicic/Adobe Stock Photos, thithawat/Adobe Stock Photos, JPchret/Adobe Stock Photos, Kadmy/Adobe Stock Photos.

Page 208: Klepikova/Adobe Stock Photos, Nikita/Adobe Stock Photos, Sylvia/Adobe Stock Photos, BortN66/Adobe Stock Photos, Tiler84/Adobe Stock Photos, gemenacom/Adobe Stock

Photos, Africa Studio/Adobe Stock Photos, ETAP/Adobe Stock Photos, abramsdesign/Adobe Stock Photos, cloud7days/ Adobe Stock Photos, Tanya Rozhnovskaya/Adobe Stock Photos, gennadiy75/Adobe Stock Photos.

Page 209: Tania Zbrodko/Adobe Stock Photos, Anterovium/ Adobe Stock Photos, Yeko Photo Studio/Adobe Stock Photos, Andrzej Tokarski/Adobe Stock Photos, sombats/Adobe Stock Photos, cipariss/Adobe Stock Photos, peterschreiber.media/ Adobe Stock Photos, Schlierner/Adobe Stock Photos, IULIIA AZAROVA/Adobe Stock Photos, dechevm/Adobe Stock Photos, Sebastian Duda/Adobe Stock Photos, foxdammit/Adobe Stock Photos.

Page 210: Restyler/Adobe Stock Photos, katrin_timoff/Adobe Stock Photos, vitaly tiagunov/Adobe Stock Photos, foxdammit/ Adobe Stock Photos, Igor Kali/Adobe Stock Photos, Oleksandr Delyk/Adobe Stock Photos, manaemedia/Adobe Stock Photos.

Page 212: THX Images/Adobe Stock Photos, Akaberka/Adobe Stock Photos, ChiccoDodiFC/Adobe Stock Photos, Andrey Popov/Adobe Stock Photos, vectorfusionart/Adobe Stock Photos, razihusin/Adobe Stock Photos, countrylens/Adobe Stock Photos, WavebreakMediaMicro/Adobe Stock Photos, skumer/ Adobe Stock Photos, fifranck/Adobe Stock Photos, Shane/ Adobe Stock Photos, kovop58/Adobe Stock Photos.

Page 213: marvent/Adobe Stock Photos, Abhishek Gaurav/ Pexels, zhukovvvlad/Adobe Stock Photos, Andreas P/Adobe Stock Photos, Snapwire/Pexels, nenetus/Adobe Stock Photos, Maridav/Adobe Stock Photos, rozmarin/Adobe Stock Photos, Miceking/Adobe Stock Photos, rozmarin/Adobe Stock Photos, Touch/Adobe Stock Photos, NickR/Adobe Stock Photos.

Page 214: Olexandr/Adobe Stock Photos, master1305/Adobe Stock Photos, sportpoint/Adobe Stock Photos, WavebreakMediaMicro/Adobe Stock Photos, Stefan Schurr/Adobe Stock Photos, WavebreakMediaMicro/Adobe Stock Photos, WavebreakMediaMicro/Adobe stock, Visit Almaty/Pexels, Gorilla/Adobe Stock Photos, EdNurg/Adobe Stock Photos, allai/Adobe Stock Photos, Visions-AD/Adobe Stock Photos.

Page 215: matimix/Adobe Stock Photos, Monkey Business/Adobe Stock Photos, blueiz60/Adobe Stock Photos, luckybusiness/Adobe Stock Photos, LIGHTFIELD STUDIOS/Adobe Stock Photos, wavebreak3/Adobe Stock Photos, RobertNyholm/Adobe Stock Photos, RealCG/Adobe Stock Photos, pololia/Adobe Stock Photos, pongsakorn_jun26/Adobe Stock Photos, mirkomedia/Adobe Stock Photos, sahua d/Adobe Stock Photos.

Page 216: Monkey Business/Adobe Stock Photos, Marino Bocelli/Adobe Stock Photos, Pexels/9145 images/Pixabay, auspicious/Adobe Stock Photos, Roman/Adobe Stock Photos, yanlev/Adobe Stock Photos, WavebreakMediaMicro/Adobe stock, matimix/Adobe Stock Photos, anekoho/Adobe Stock Photos, Drobot Dean/Adobe Stock Photos, Nestor/Adobe Stock Photos, EvgeniiAnd/Adobe Stock Photos.

Page 218: Dusan Kostic/Adobe Stock Photos, Siarhei Kulikou/Adobe Stock Photos, novoselov/Adobe Stock Photos, tunedin/Adobe Stock Photos, _italo_/Adobe Stock Photos, olly/Adobe Stock Photos, tarasov_vl/Adobe Stock Photos, SFIO CRACHO/Adobe Stock Photos, Nicholas Piccillo/Adobe Stock Photos, AHMAD FAIZAL YAHYA/Adobe Stock Photos, RobertNyholm/Adobe Stock Photos, WavebreakMediaMicro/Adobe Stock Photos.

Page 219: photology1971/Adobe Stock Photos, Alexander Y/Adobe Stock Photos.

Page 220: SGr/Adobe Stock Photos, frinz/Adobe Stock Photos, jc/Adobe Stock Photos, goodluz/Adobe Stock Photos, Yay Images/Adobe Stock Photos, mma23/Adobe Stock Photos, topshots/Adobe Stock Photos, naraichal/Adobe Stock Photos, haveseen/Adobe Stock Photos, Rostislav Ageev/Adobe Stock Photos, Tyler Olson/Adobe Stock Photos, Kzenon/Adobe Stock Photos.

Page 221: Ammit/Adobe Stock Photos.

Page 222: Artem Furman/Adobe Stock Photos, Denis Rozhnovsky/Adobe Stock Photos, Paulista/Adobe Stock Photos, artem_goncharov/Adobe Stock Photos, Gowtham/Adobe Stock

Photos, auremar/Adobe Stock Photos, Tyler Olson/Adobe Stock Photos, Christos Georghiou/Adobe Stock Photos, IvicaNS/Adobe Stock Photos, HjIFTINA/Adobe Stock Photos, Balint Radu/Adobe Stock Photos, Andrey Burmakin/Adobe Stock Photos.

Page 223: Michael/Adobe Stock Photos, Sonulkaster/Adobe Stock Photos, danielegay/Adobe Stock Photos, PaHa/Adobe Stock Photos, artem_goncharov/Adobe Stock Photos, กรบุรษ วรดี/Adobe Stock Photos, ponomarencko/Adobe Stock Photos, nicoletaionescu/Adobe Stock Photos, nicoletaionescu/Adobe Stock Photos, Pavel Losevsky/Adobe Stock Photos, MagicalKrew/Adobe Stock Photos, Gorodenkoff/Adobe Stock Photos.

Page 224: Mark Poprocki/Adobe Stock Photos, AntonioDiaz/Adobe Stock Photos, zinkevych/Adobe Stock Photos, nadia_snopek/Adobe Stock Photos, David Fuentes/Adobe Stock Photos, Evelien/Adobe Stock Photos, auremar/Adobe Stock Photos, Ariadna de Raadt/Adobe Stock Photos.

Page 225: gnepphoto/Adobe Stock Photos, guruXOX/Adobe Stock Photos.

Page 226: metamorworks/Adobe Stock Photos, andrys lukowski/Adobe Stock Photos, carlosgardel/Adobe Stock Photos, Thomas Pajot/Adobe Stock Photos, Pasc06/Adobe Stock Photos, Anton Gvozdikov/Adobe Stock Photos, julialine802/Adobe Stock Photos, olenaari/Adobe Stock Photos, Ruslan/Adobe Stock Photos, itestro/Adobe Stock Photos, Riccardo Meloni/Adobe Stock Photos, kozlik_mozlik/Adobe Stock Photos.

Page 227: phonlamaiphoto/Adobe Stock Photos, andrys lukowski/Adobe Stock Photos, melnikofd/Adobe Stock Photos, New Africa/Adobe Stock Photos, eissfeldtk/2 images/Pixabay, WavebreakMediaMicro/Adobe Stock Photos, Andrey Lapshin/Adobe Stock Photos, aerogondo/Adobe Stock Photos, ZoneCreative/Adobe Stock Photos, Yay Images/Adobe Stock Photos, Pixel-Shot/Adobe Stock Photos, Sergey Bogdanov/Adobe Stock Photos.

Page 228: auremar/Adobe Stock Photos, andreysafonov/Adobe Stock Photos, Daddy Cool/Adobe Stock Photos, Ricardo Ferrando/Adobe Stock Photos, marqs/Adobe Stock Photos, Alex/Adobe Stock Photos, LoloStock/Adobe Stock Photos, WavebreakMediaMicro/Adobe Stock Photos, elen31/Adobe Stock Photos, andrys lukowski/Adobe Stock Photos, moodboard/Adobe Stock Photos, auremar/Adobe Stock Photos.

Page 229: seandeburca/Adobe Stock Photos, Anna Jurkovska/Adobe Stock Photos, kozlik_mozlik/Adobe Stock Photos, kozlik_mozlik/Adobe Stock Photos.

Page 230: Gary/Adobe Stock Photos, kivi80/Adobe Stock Photos, vitaliy_melnik/Adobe Stock Photos, melnikofd/Adobe Stock Photos, ramirezom/Adobe Stock Photos, Thomas Pajot/Adobe Stock Photos, Laura Lévy/Adobe Stock Photos, aerogondo/Adobe Stock Photos, Andrey Lapshin/Adobe Stock Photos, silvae/Adobe Stock Photos, rost9/Adobe Stock Photos, James Steidl/Adobe Stock Photos.

Page 231: WikimediaImages/5817 images/Pixabay, Pavel Losevsky/Adobe Stock Photos, 18percentgrey/Adobe Stock Photos, Kalim/Adobe Stock Photos, WikimediaImages/5817 images/Pixabay, Fred Rullman/Wikmedia Commons, One/Adobe Stock Photos, Giuseppe Verdi/Wikimedia commons, BenFrantzDale/Flickr, andrys lukowski/Adobe Stock Photos, kozlik_mozlik/Adobe Stock Photos.

Page 232: Kalim/Adobe Stock Photos, Voice of America/Wikimedia commons, kozlik_mozlik/Adobe Stock Photos, kozlik_mozlik/Adobe Stock Photos, ehretkorea/1 image/Pixabay, artesitalia/10 images/Pixabay, caifas/Adobe Stock Photos, Jan Rose/Adobe Stock Photos, Svyatoslav Lypynskyy/Adobe Stock Photos, denebola_h/Adobe Stock Photos.

Page 234: Monkey Business/Adobe Stock Photos, 4th Life Photography/Adobe Stock Photos, 4th Life Photography/Adobe Stock Photos, Pavel Losevsky/Adobe Stock Photos, Andriy Blokhin/Adobe Stock Photos, Olga Kovalenko/Adobe Stock Photos, Mariakray/Adobe Stock Photos, Sandor Kacso/Adobe Stock Photos, DedMityay/Adobe Stock Photos, 4th Life Photography/Adobe Stock Photos, auremar/Adobe Stock Photos, Monkey Business/Adobe Stock Photos.

Page 235: Monkey Business/Adobe Stock Photos, Vladislav Gajic/Adobe Stock Photos, kaboompics/961 images/Pixabay, Jeffery/Adobe Stock Photos, golubovy/Adobe Stock Photos, WikiImages/1175 images/Pixabay, Brian Jackson/Adobe Stock Photos, anczika/Adobe Stock Photos, diego cervo/Adobe Stock Photos, xia/Adobe Stock Photos, Maksym Protsenko/Adobe Stock Photos, Travel_Master/Adobe Stock Photos.

Page 236: jorisvo/Adobe Stock Photos, nathings/Adobe Stock Photos, Mari Dein/Adobe Stock Photos, cascoly2/Adobe Stock Photos, leungchopan/Adobe Stock Photos, olly/Adobe Stock Photos, Photographee.eu/Adobe Stock Photos, Monkey Business/Adobe Stock Photos, auremar/Adobe Stock Photos, 4th Life Photography/Adobe Stock Photos.

Page 238: radenmas/Adobe Stock Photos, Marina/Adobe Stock Photos, sansara/iStock/Getty Images, ThorstenF / 472 images, ewela_s/Adobe Stock Photos, Pavel Losevsky/Adobe Stock Photos, takazart/360 images/Pixabay, Imagine Corp/Adobe Stock Photos, Africa Studio/Adobe Stock Photos, James Steidl/ Adobe Stock Photos, AGCuesta/Adobe Stock Photos, vetkit/ Adobe Stock Photos.

Page 239: Sergey Lavrentev/Adobe Stock Photos, Erica Guilane-Nachez/Adobe Stock Photos, Leonidovich/Adobe Stock Photos, milkovasa/Adobe Stock Photos, ARTYuSTUDIO/Adobe Stock Photos, alephcomo1/Adobe Stock Photos, dino4ka2020/ Adobe Stock Photos, 3drenderings/Adobe Stock Photos, maxmann/808 images/Pixabay, small tom/Adobe Stock Photos, Andrey Popov/Adobe Stock Photos, paulmz/Adobe Stock Photos.

Page 240: AGCuesta/Adobe Stock Photos, Dimitrius/Adobe Stock Photos, venusangel/Adobe Stock Photos, small tom/ Adobe Stock Photos, alephcomo1/Adobe Stock Photos, BillionPhotos.com/Adobe Stock Photos, TimurD/Adobe Stock Photos, nahariyani100/Adobe Stock Photos, PBaishev/Adobe Stock Photos, mipan/Adobe Stock Photos, borisblik/Adobe Stock Photos, Илья Бурдун/Adobe Stock Photos.

Page 241: yevhen_holovash/Adobe Stock Photos, aleksandarfilip/Adobe Stock Photos, Nikolai Sorokin/Adobe Stock Photos, crushmaster/Adobe Stock Photos, alexsol/Adobe Stock Photos, Aarrttuurr/Adobe Stock Photos, sapsan777/Adobe Stock Photos, Glenda Powers/Adobe Stock Photos, Tony Baggett/ Adobe Stock Photos, frank peters/Adobe Stock Photos, kelifamily/Adobe Stock Photos, emily2k/Adobe Stock Photos.

Page 242: Artem Furman/Adobe Stock Photos, AntonioDiaz/ Adobe Stock Photos, Smileus/Adobe Stock Photos, bigjom/ Adobe Stock Photos, twinsterphoto/Adobe Stock Photos, New Africa/Adobe Stock Photos, stokkete/Adobe Stock Photos, mariesacha/Adobe Stock Photos, ChiccoDodiFC/Adobe Stock Photos, igor_kell/Adobe Stock Photos, ieang/Adobe Stock Photos.

Chapter 07

Page 246: SciePro/Adobe Stock Photos, Benjamin Gelman/ Adobe Stock Photos, Romario Ien/Adobe Stock Photos, PIC4U/ Adobe Stock Photos, Anatomy Insider/Adobe Stock Photos, microcozm/Adobe Stock Photos, paisan191/Adobe Stock Photos, Rido/Adobe Stock Photos, simmittorok/Adobe Stock Photos, eranicle/Adobe Stock Photos, ag visuell/Adobe Stock Photos, kei907/Adobe Stock Photos.

Page 247: vladimirfloyd/Adobe Stock Photos, mraoraor/Adobe Stock Photos, razoomanetu/Adobe Stock Photos, LoloStock/ Adobe Stock Photos, Brother's Art/Adobe Stock Photos, HANK GREBE/Adobe Stock Photos, adimas/Adobe Stock Photos, alexlmx/Adobe Stock Photos, Evgen/Adobe Stock Photos, Sagittaria/Adobe Stock Photos, dream@do/Adobe Stock Photos, yodiyim/Adobe Stock Photos.

Page 248: 2dmolier/Adobe Stock Photos, rommma/Adobe Stock Photos, SciePro/Adobe Stock Photos, Maksym Yemelyanov/Adobe Stock Photos, javiindy/Adobe Stock Photos, puhhha/Adobe Stock Photos, littlestocker/Adobe Stock Photos, exzozis/Adobe Stock Photos, filistimlyanin1/Adobe Stock Photos, mraoraor/Adobe Stock Photos, Krakenimages.com/Adobe Stock Photos, Alex/Adobe Stock Photos.

Page 249: Zemler/Adobe Stock Photos, Krakenimages.com/ Adobe Stock Photos, kaymotec/Adobe Stock Photos, yellowj/

Adobe Stock Photos, Photographee.eu/Adobe Stock Photos, mraoraor/Adobe Stock Photos, SciePro/Adobe Stock Photos, iulianvalentin/Adobe Stock Photos, WavebreakMediaMicro/ Adobe Stock Photos, Glebstock/Adobe Stock Photos, vladimir-floyd/Adobe Stock Photos, Glebstock/Adobe Stock Photos.

Page 250: Angelika Smile/Adobe Stock Photos, Antonioguillem/ Adobe Stock Photos, pixelaway/Adobe Stock Photos, Fotos 593/Adobe Stock Photos, Helder Sousa/Adobe Stock Photos, el_buruc/Adobe Stock Photos.

Page 251: narongchaihlaw/Adobe Stock Photos, rufar/Adobe Stock Photos, hans12/Adobe Stock Photos, Syda Productions/ Adobe Stock Photos, ninell/Adobe Stock Photos, Liudmila Dutko/Adobe Stock Photos, marinafrost/Adobe Stock Photos, marinafrost/Adobe Stock Photos, elavuk81/Adobe Stock Photos, Kurhan/Adobe Stock Photos, New Africa/Adobe Stock Photos, DragonFly/Adobe Stock Photos.

Page 252: WavebreakMediaMicro/Adobe Stock Photos, Ovcharenko/Adobe Stock Photos, batke82as/Adobe Stock Photos, PixieMe/Adobe Stock Photos, elen31/Adobe Stock Photos, schankz/Adobe Stock Photos, booleen/Adobe Stock Photos, Syda Productions/Adobe Stock Photos.

Page 253: bnenin/Adobe Stock Photos, didesign/Adobe Stock Photos, photowahn/Adobe Stock Photos, Racle Fotodesign/ Adobe Stock Photos, Vitalii Vodolazskyi/Adobe Stock Photos, drubig-photo/Adobe Stock Photos, sebra/Adobe Stock Photos, Ольга Тернавская/Adobe Stock Photos, rogerphoto/Adobe Stock Photos, studiopure/Adobe Stock Photos, Sherry Young/ Adobe Stock Photos, Aleksandra Suzi/Adobe Stock Photos.

Page 254: Andrey Popov/Adobe Stock Photos, artem_goncharov/Adobe Stock Photos, Sven Vietense/Adobe Stock Photos, stockartstudio/Adobe Stock Photos, piXuLariUm/Adobe Stock Photos, JGade/Adobe Stock Photos, alexmak/Adobe Stock Photos, Otto/Adobe Stock Photos, Simone van den Berg/Adobe Stock Photos, Lisa F. Young/Adobe Stock Photos, master1305/ Adobe Stock Photos, Racle Fotodesign/Adobe Stock Photos.

Page 255: Racle Fotodesign/Adobe Stock Photos, gallofilm/ Adobe Stock Photos, BillionPhotos.com/Adobe Stock Photos, michaelheim/Adobe Stock Photos, Kaspars Grinvalds/Adobe Stock Photos, Photographee.eu/Adobe Stock Photos, zinkevych/Adobe Stock Photos, sebra/Adobe Stock Photos, tugolukof/Adobe Stock Photos, RFBSIP/Adobe Stock Photos, Andrey Popov/Adobe Stock Photos.

Page 257: Tyler Olson/Adobe Stock Photos, Andy Dean/Adobe Stock Photos, Kadmy/Adobe Stock Photos, BestForYou/Adobe Stock Photos, dimasobko/Adobe Stock Photos, Winai Tepsuttinun/Adobe Stock Photos, Stefano Garau/Adobe Stock Photos, Dario Lo Presti/Adobe Stock Photos, photophonie/Adobe Stock Photos, Voyagerix/Adobe Stock Photos, Andrzej Wilusz/Adobe Stock Photos, Coprid/Adobe Stock Photos.

Page 258: blackday/Adobe Stock Photos, gna60/Adobe Stock Photos, Tsuboya/Adobe Stock Photos, Getty Images, TKBstudio/Adobe Stock Photos, filistimlyanin1/Adobe Stock Photos, sebra/Adobe Stock Photos, Xuejun li/Adobe Stock Photos, Friends Stock/Adobe Stock Photos, guerrieroale/Adobe Stock Photos.

Page 259: upixa/Adobe Stock Photos, xiaosan/Adobe Stock Photos, Robert Hainer/Adobe Stock Photos, WavebreakMediaMicro/Adobe Stock Photos, rocketclips/Adobe Stock Photos, luckybusiness/Adobe Stock Photos, diego cervo/Adobe Stock Photos, zeremskimilan/Adobe Stock Photos, endostock/Adobe Stock Photos, thodonal/Adobe Stock Photos, romaset/Adobe Stock Photos, rh2010/Adobe Stock Photos.

Page 260: Tyler Olson/Adobe Stock Photos, Jacob Lund/Adobe Stock Photos, Rainer Fuhrmann/Adobe Stock Photos, Oksana_S/Adobe Stock Photos, snesivan/Adobe Stock Photos, Gennadiy Poznyakov/Adobe Stock Photos, amawasri/Adobe Stock Photos, pixelheadphoto/Adobe Stock Photos, decade3d/Adobe Stock Photos, Liliia/Adobe Stock Photos, Africa Studio/Adobe Stock Photos, Andrey Popov/Adobe Stock Photos.

Page 261: terovesalainen/Adobe Stock Photos, Liza5450/Adobe Stock Photos, HSN/Adobe Stock Photos, bunyos/Adobe Stock Photos, shutterdemon/Adobe Stock Photos, zinkevych/Adobe Stock Photos, pixelaway/Adobe Stock Photos, kleberpicui/Adobe Stock Photos, Daisy Daisy/Adobe Stock Photos, sunnysky69/Adobe Stock Photos.

Page 263: LIGHTFIELD STUDIOS/Adobe Stock Photos, [illegible] mank76/Adobe Stock Photos, seanlockephotography/Adobe Stock Photos, David San Segundo/Adobe Stock Photos, Noel/ Adobe Stock Photos, Nikolai Sorokin/Fotolia, robtek/Adobe Stock Photos, Ad van Brunschot/Adobe Stock Photos, ompho-to/Adobe Stock Photos, Lisa F. Young/Adobe Stock Photos, iofo-to/Adobe Stock Photos, boonchuay1970/Adobe Stock Photos.

Page 264: scphoto48/Adobe Stock Photos, Korta/Adobe Stock Photos, pressmaster/Adobe Stock Photos, exclusive-design/ Adobe Stock Photos, Witthaya/Adobe Stock Photos, fpic/ Adobe Stock Photos, graversen36/Adobe Stock Photos, Adobe Systems Incorporated, Photographee.eu/Adobe Stock Photos, Andrey Popov/Adobe Stock Photos, Andre Bonn/Adobe Stock Photos, goro20/Adobe Stock Photos.

Page 265: donserhio/Adobe Stock Photos, Peter Kim/Adobe Stock Photos, zoka74/Adobe Stock Photos, Shawn Hempel/ Adobe Stock Photos, Lisa F. Young/Adobe Stock Photos, Moni-ka Wisniewska/Adobe Stock Photos, hafakot/Adobe Stock Pho-tos, Kzenon/Adobe Stock Photos, Bits and Splits/Adobe Stock Photos, Photobeps/Adobe Stock Photos, MclittleStock/Adobe Stock Photos, Jane/Adobe Stock Photos.

Page 266: Luevanos/Adobe Stock Photos, phatanin17/Adobe Stock Photos, Photographee.eu/Adobe Stock Photos, Photo_Ma/Adobe Stock Photos, Photographee.eu/Adobe Stock Pho-tos, VadimGuzhva/Adobe Stock Photos, ownza/Adobe Stock Photos, Photographee.eu/Adobe Stock Photos, graja/Adobe Stock Photos, Rafael Ben-Ari/Adobe Stock Photos.

Page 268: Tyler Olson/Adobe Stock Photos, marilyn barbone/ Adobe Stock Photos, Kadmy/Adobe Stock Photos, freedom_na-ruk/Adobe Stock Photos, Jackson Pearson/Adobe Stock Pho-tos, zimmytws/Adobe Stock Photos, subhanbaghirov/Adobe Stock Photos, Ildar Sagdejev/Wikimedia Commons, Robert Wil-son/Adobe Stock Photos, Rawpixel.com/Adobe Stock Photos, markobe/Adobe Stock Photos, 22091967/Adobe Stock Photos.

Page 269: peter armstrong/Adobe Stock Photos, shocky/Adobe Stock Photos, Gorodenkoff/Adobe Stock Photos, Andrey Po-pov/Adobe Stock Photos.